Thought and Feeling

Thought and Feeling

Cognitive Alteration of Feeling States

Edited by Harvey London
and Richard E. Nisbett

Routledge
Taylor & Francis Group
LONDON AND NEW YORK

First published 1974 by Transaction Publishers

Published 2017 by Routledge
2 Park Square, Milton Park, Abingdon, Oxon OX14 4RN
711 Third Avenue, New York, NY 10017, USA

First issued in hardback 2017

Routledge is an imprint of the Taylor & Francis Group, an informa business

Library of Congress Catalog Number: 2007026455

Library of Congress Cataloging-in-Publication Data

Thought and feeling : cognitive alteration of feeling states / [edited by] Harvey London and Richard E. Nisbett.
p. cm.
Originally published: Chicago : Aldine Pub. Co., 1974.
Includes bibliographical references and index.
ISBN 978-0-202-36176-5 (alk. paper)
1. Emotions and cognition. 2. Heider, Fritz, 1896- 3. Schachter, Stanley, 1922- I. London, Harvey. II. Nisbett, Richard E.

BF311.T486 2007
153--dc22

2007026455

ISBN 13: 978-1-138-53964-8 (hbk)
ISBN 13: 978-0-202-36176-5 (pbk)

To Our Parents and Our Wives

Contents

Contributors

T. X. Barber, *Medfield Foundation*
John C. Barefoot, *Carleton University*
Aaron Beck, *University of Pennsylvania*
Daryl J. Bem, *Stanford University*
Leonard Berkowitz, *University of Wisconsin*
Melvin Crosby, *Clark University*
Kermit Henriksen, *University of New Mexico*
George O. Klemp, *University of Wisconsin*
Karl P. Koenig, *University of New Mexico*
James Laird, *Clark University*
Gerald Lang, *Boston University*
Howard Leventhal, *University of Wisconsin*
Harvey London, *Long Island University*
Brendan Maher, *Harvard University*
Lenore Monello, *Brandeis University*
Richard E. Nisbett, *University of Michigan*
Edgar O'Neal, *Tulane University*
Jerome E. Singer, *State University of New York, Stony Brook*
Nicholas P. Spanos, *Boston University*
Michael D. Storms, *University of Kansas*
Ronald B. Straub, *Dartmouth University*
Charles Turner, *University of Wisconsin*
Stuart Valins, *State University of New York, Stony Brook*

Contributors

Thought and Feeling

I

Introduction

1

Jerome E. Singer

Historical Background

James T. Farrell reportedly once defined a sociologist as a man who spends $100,000 to find a whorehouse. If psychologists find that canard funny, it only hurts when they laugh, for they too are often accused, and frequently correctly, of discovering and elaborating the obvious. We must ruefully acknowledge that much of our labors consist of confirmations of the commonplace, and there is a touch of irony in the recognition that sometimes simple, common sense, but highly important observations about human functioning are almost completely ignored.

Recently, there has been a growing awareness and acceptance of such a straightforward but neglected proposition: people do not exist in a world of physically defined forces and events; they live in a world defined by their own perceptions, cognitions, conclusions, and imaginations. That is, a person responds to and reacts to, not some objective or experimenter-defined set of stimuli, but to his apperceptions and subjectively-defined stimuli. Specific cases of this rather simple statement are easy to document. For example, in an experiment on verbal clustering and free recall, where one of the experimental conditions contains a sentence in its instructions designed to make the subject cognizant of an interrelationship between the words on the list, it makes a difference whether or not the subject attends to and comprehends the sentence. If he does, there is an experiment; if not, there is no subjective difference between the experimental and control instructions.

Obviously, no proposition, let alone one as simple as the one stated above arises without roots or predecessors, and it is not hard to find even influential statements of that nature in modern social psychology. Lewin's development of the life space and W. I. Thomas' nominalism would certainly qualify. Yet, in their own way, each of those positions failed to carry the day. Thomas, a sociologist, was never a major influence in psychological circles and Lewin's formulations, while certainly pivotal developments, were partially assimilated into the general S-R climate and were even classified as learning theories by major summarizers and textbooks. Behaviorism and the S-R climate, which for many years were couched in an extremely narrow language, were certainly factors in obscuring the obvious.

The primary influence in bringing what is now called attribution theory to the attention of contemporary social psychologists was Fritz Heider. His major work, *The Psychology of Interpersonal Relations* (1958), although well-known for its discussions of balance and cognitive consistency, has attribution as its focus. Heider centers his discussion on the naive psychologist, that is, the man in the street, and how he relates his inferences about the world and his actions to his attributions about causality and intent. Consider a man hit on the head by a coconut. If the nut merely falls from the tree, the man probably will not attribute sentience or intent to the tree--no matter what remedial action he takes. If, on the other hand, a person in the tree dropped the coconut, the droppee may well attribute awareness and intent to the dropper, interpret the same physical situation, a coconut with mass m and velocity v striking the top of his head, in a different fashion, and react in completely different ways.

One always feels a bit foolish talking about the general case of attribution, for just as Moliere's *Le Bourgeois Gentilhomme* spoke prose all his life without realizing it, so have we all been attributing all of our lives. The very act of interpreting the world and making inferences before acting is so commonplace that once it is defined as attribution, other than remarking, "So that's what you call it," very little else can or need be said. The situations in which attribution becomes interesting are those in which there is an effect produced by a misattribution or a change in attribution. When a person behaves in what is considered a normal or routine fashion in a particular situation, no one pays much attention. When the person behaves in an unorthodox or unusual way in the same set of circumstances, he is the subject of discussion. But if his abnormal or aberrant behavior can be explained as a result of his idiosyncratic attribution of causality, then he becomes the genesis of a case study or experiment.

Some of the intriguing aspects of attribution have been outlined in review articles by Kelley (1967) and by Jones and Davis (1965). They have summarized the operational aspects of the theory, codified previous research, including many seemingly disparate studies, and shown how some of their own work extends the theory. Yet, for those who are not familiar with these articles, an illustration of attribution theory might be useful. Certainly the most graphic of the exponents of attribution theory was Walt Disney, whose motion picture *Dumbo* represents a classic of the genre. Dumbo is the titular hero of an animated cartoon motion picture. He is a small, young elephant with very large ears. Eliding those aspects of the plot not of relevance to the point at issue, it develops that Dumbo, while asleep, can fly, by flapping his ears like a bird's wings. When awake, he is land bound, just like any other elephant; his friends, the birds, are unable to persuade the nonsomnulent Dumbo that he is that unlikely creature, a flying elephant. One of the birds eventually plucks a routine feather from among those covering his own rump. He presents it to Dumbo together with an elaborate story which describes the feather as a magical one. The feather purportedly has the power of enabling its bearer to fly; to lend plausibility Dumbo is told that the magic feather is the means by which birds teach their young to aviate. Dumbo accepts the gift and attributes flying-inducing power to the feather. Holding it in his trunk, he is able to fly. Eventually, Dumbo loses the feather and once again, is unable to voluntarily fly. When his friends are, at last, able to convince him that the feather was not really magical, Dumbo is finally able to fly by himself.

Dumbo's experiences represent an interesting example of attribution. In the first state, although he possessed the capacity to fly, he was unable to attribute that talent to himself, and, hence, could not fly. When given the feather and misattributing the flying power to its magic rather than to his own improbable capabilities, he actually flies rather well. Later, when he is confronted with the facts that he has flown and that his attribution of the cause to the feather was incorrect, he is able to attribute correctly the talent to himself and to fly without external props. The intervening misattribution accomplished a persuasive task that was not possible merely with the evidence available to the senses. *Dumbo*, of course, is a fictional work filled with literary hyperbole. Yet, without straining, we can make the analogy: If attribution theory can persuade a cartoon elephant that he can fly by flapping his ears, imagine its power when applied to real life human beings.

The present volume is a collection of papers centering on one aspect of the attribution process: the extent to which the attribution of events and causes results in the determination, modification or alteration of emotions, feelings and affective state. Not all of the papers are couched in terms of attribution, but all of them refer to the processes included in the term. Just as misattribution represents an especially interesting aspect of the more general attribution processes, the realm of feelings and emotions and the interplay of the physiological and cognitive factors underlying them are equally fascinating. For both a tradition of psychobiological research and of common sense would have us believe that such experiences as anger, joy, fear, love, etc., are simply determined outcomes of basic central nervous system stimulation. Indeed, some physiologically oriented motivation theorists would almost have us believe that if enough electrodes, properly implanted in the hypothalamus and other parts of the limbic system, were connected to a keyboard, the psychologist could play a human as if he were a pipe organ, orchestrating his emotions and their associated reactions at will. Out of such fantasies are science fiction movies made, yet, they are demonstrably inadequate.

A growing body of literature and many psychologists

now attest to the view that feelings and emotions, in human beings, are as much a function of the person's evaluation and appraisal of his environment as they are of immediate predisposing physiological factors. There is, in fact, a contemporary set of theories that holds that all human functioning is a type of information processing. A person receives signals and stimuli from various sources--some peripheral, some central, some self-generated, some environmentally produced--and his appraisal of them and consequent behavior is determined by their resultant. Thus in order for a person to be angry he will need two inputs, the physiological concomitants of anger and the cognition that his environmental setting is an appropriate one for anger. This is not the place for a summary of the literature on anger, but there is evidence that this formulation is applicable to animals other than humans, that is, animals whose cognitive capacities are not all that refined. The general notion that stimuli, including reinforcements, are primarily sources of information is now as respectable a view in comparative psychology as it is in social psychology.

All of this has some interesting implications for attribution. For if various forms of information are to be processed as a precursor to action or even to feeling, there are several places at which this information may be modified. The stimulus itself may be changed; the perception and attention to the stimulus may be modified; the appraisal of the meaning, value and, in some cases, intent, of the stimulus may be altered. It is to that third situation that most of attribution is addressed. For example, when a woman wakes up nauseous and with a headache, her feelings, and possibly actions, will be different depending upon whether she interprets her physical state as pregnancy or a hangover. The stimuli are interpreted as equivalent and in both cases she is attending to them. It is her appraisal, that is, her attribution of cause, which makes all the difference. And, under some circumstances, she may not even appraise her physiological symptoms as medically related.

Perhaps the underlying conceptual schemes can be bet ter illustrated with experimental rather than hypothetical examples. Several years ago, Stanley Schachter and

I (1962) conducted an experiment which, although not couched in attribution terminology, incorporates most of the salient features of the theory. For simplicity of exposition, I shall leave out some of the details and one control condition; the description will be somewhat idealized, but more germane to the present discussion. When each subject for the experiment arrived at the laboratory, he was told that the study was one exploring the effects of a vitamin compound, Suproxin, upon vision. A physician proceeded to give him a subcutaneous injection of Suproxin, and then the subject was informed that there would be a 15-20 minute waiting period to allow time for the compound to be absorbed into the bloodstream before the visual testing could be held. A second subject, supposedly also Suproxin-injected but actually an experimental confederate, was brought into the room to pass the waiting time with the real subject. After the waiting period, the experimenter re-entered the room and administered a set of questionaires. Following the completion of the forms, the experiment was ended; the subject was given an explanation of the purposes and procedures of the study.

Obviously, we were not studying the effects of vitamins upon vision. What we were studying was how a person labels, or decides, whether he is undergoing an emotion, and, if so, which one. Suproxin is a fictitious word disguising different injected substances; two thirds of the subjects were actually injected with a dose of adrenalin, the remainder, with an innocuous salt water placebo. A short time after the injection, the adrenalin injected subjects experienced all the physiological symptoms of sympathomimetic stimulation, for example, hand tremors, heart pounding, rapid breathing, and so forth; the placebo-injected subjects had no such dramatic internal change. One half of the adrenalin subjects were told that Suproxin had several side effects, so that they might expect to feel trembling and heart pounding as a result of the injection. The rest of the adrenalin subjects and the placebo subjects were told nothing about Suproxin's side effects.

During the time the subject and the confederate were waiting, allegedly for the Suproxin to enter the blood stream, the confederate engaged in a preset pattern of conversation and behavior. With one half of the subjects, he became progressively more angry at the experiment, the experimenter, and an interim questionnaire he and the subject were completing; with the other half, he became more and more euphoric and playful. During this interval, the subject was observed through a one-way vision screen and his behavior was systematically recorded and coded for instances of either anger or euphoria. The final questionnaires, administered after the waiting period, elicited self-reports from the subjects about their physiological and emotional state.

The whole point of what may seem to the reader to be a rather elaborate charade was an attempt to assess the conditions under which people become emotional and report their emotion. In summary, the experimental procedure created six different groups of subjects. They differed in the amount and kinds of information available to them.

A. Placebo-injected subjects placed with an angry confederate.
B. Placebo-injected subjects placed with a euphoric confederate.

These two groups had no especial physiological activation, that is, no internal information about being aroused.

C. Adrenalin-injected subjects placed with an angry confederate.
D. Adrenalin-injected subjects placed with a euphoric confederate.

These two groups had a degree of physiological activation, that is, internal information that they were aroused, but no information about the genesis or the interpretation of this arousal.

E. Adrenalin-injected subjects placed with an angry confederate and told that Suproxin had activating side effects.
F. Adrenalin-injected subjects placed with a euphoric confederate and told that Suproxin had activating side effects.

These two groups had a degree of physiological activation, that is, internal information that they were aroused, plus additional information about the source of and reason for this arousal.

The results are particularly cogent to the theories underlying most of the studies in this volume. The first two groups (A and B) did not become emotional. Not having arousal, they had nothing to attribute, and hence made no attribution that influenced their behavior; they became neither angry nor euphoric. The second two groups (C and D) became emotional. Those subjects with the angry confederate became angry; those with the euphoric stooge became euphoric. Both groups of subjects had identical kinds of arousal and no specific attribution of its causality. The subjects presumably observed the confederate and interpreted his behavior in informational terms: anger or euphoria was called for in the situation, was appropriate, and was probably what had aroused them; therefore, they were angry or euphoric. The last two groups (E and F) did not become emotional, neither angry nor euphoric. Even though they were aroused, they had information enabling them to attribute causality for their activation. Quite simply, the Suproxin caused it. They had no need for the additional information provided by the confederate's behavior and they did not make an attribution based on it. In context, the conclusion is that an emotion is neither a physiological event determined by factors under the skin nor is it determined by environmental events impinging upon the person. Rather, it is the result of a complex evaluation of internal and external pieces of information and is particularly affected by a person's attributions of the causality, intent, and extent of these factors.

The emotion experiment, just described, is a model for the studies that follow in two ways. First, the general interest in attribution, with particular reference to emotions and feeling states, and the interplay of their cognitive and physiological antecedents, is a theme that is explored by most of the contributors. Second, the particular view of the emotional process developed by Schachter and his co-workers about this study and several subsequent ones is the major groundwork for the theory underlying many of the contributions. In simplest, perhaps even oversimplified terms, an emotion or emotional behavior occurs when both physiological and cognitive information indicate that it is appropriate and when the necessary attributions can be made. From that as a start, interesting questions can be asked. For example, does the physiological information have to come from real physiological sources, or can a person receive the same knowledge through cognitive channels? That is, just as poor Mr. Bunbury, in *The Importance of Being Earnest*, was dying because his doctor told him he was dying and he had great faith in his doctor, perhaps external reports of a person's physical state can supplement or override the real thing.

The conception that an emotion is based on evaluation of information and attribution does not specify the ways in which the assessment is to be made. Different investigators have different views and the spectrum of mechanisms for the operation of attribution runs from radical behaviorism through general cognitive theory to medical models. The issue is far from being settled. It is one of those fortunate intellectual disagreements which not only does not impede research, but actually stimulates it.

To recapitulate, the present volume contains a series of studies, cognitively oriented, which fit into a current atmosphere of research utilizing attribution. They all investigate facets of the process by which various kinds of information, both cognitive and physiological, are appraised and amalgamated by an individual. The particular type of research was illustrated by an attribution study that provided both an experimental paradigm and a theoretical stance. The studies which follow will collectively refine, modify, and develop this initial statement.

NOTE

1. The preparation of this chapter was supported, in part, by Grant GS-2412 from the National Science Foundation.

REFERENCES

Heider, F. 1958. *The Psychology of Interpersonal Relations*. New York: Wiley.

Jones, E.E., and Davis, K.E. 1965. From Acts to Dispositions. *In* L. Berkowitz (ed.), *Advances in Experimental Social Psychology*, Vol. 2. New York:

Academic Press.
Kelley, H.H. 1967. Attribution Theory in Social Psychology. *In* D. Levine (ed.), *Nebraska Symposium on Motivation*, Vol. 15. Lincoln: University of Nebraska Press.
Schachter, S., and Singer, J.E. 1962. Cognitive, social and physiological determinants of emotional state. *Psychological Review* 69:379-399.

2

Harvey London and
Richard E. Nisbett

Elements of Schachter's Cognitive Theory of Emotional States

Any theory of elegance and power is bound to stimulate research which exemplifies, extends, clarifies, and even attacks the original statement of the theory. It is useful to see such research in one place, so that the intellectual points scored play upon each other, weaving a pattern simultaneously more complex and more lucid than usually results from scattered publication in a variety of journals.

We here bring together a variety of studies, each of which tackles some facet of the theory of emotion enunciated by Stanley Schachter and Jerome Singer (1962) and further developed by Schachter (1964, 1971). The theory, which postulates interaction of cognitive and physiological factors to bring about an emotional state, is outlined by Singer in the chapter on historical background. This book shows how various investigators have used elements of the theory to aid in understanding psychopathology, aggression, eating behavior, the halo effect, and a variety of other behaviors.

It will be useful, for purposes of introducing and organizing the book, to state Schachter's theory yet once again in terms of its primary elements. The theory may be schematized in the following way: (1) an *internal cue* (2) *arouses evaluative needs*. The evaluative needs lead, in turn, to a (3) *process of explanation* in terms of (4) an *external cue*. The end result of these steps is, of course, an emotional state.

This formulation by Schachter was not intended to state the way emotions arise invariably or even often. Schachter admits that emotions often arise differently (1971:2). For example, in nature an external cue may give rise to internal cues (the sudden appearance of a bear may trigger autonomic arousal), and an emotion may result immediately without any "evaluative needs" having arisen or a "process of explanation" having been initiated.

What the formulation does make clear is the distinction between internal and external sources of emotional states and the specification of cognitive processes which link and alter the two. The formulation leads readily to experimental procedures designed to separately manipulate and measure internal cues, external cues, and the cognitive processes which mediate them.

Distinguishing the elements of Schachter's theory as we have done raises fundamental definition and process questions about the various elements. What may serve as an internal cue? When do evaluative needs arise and when do they not? What is the nature of the process of explanation? What may serve as an external cue? How do the various elements interact? The studies presented here speak to each of these questions. Let us preview the studies to see what they have to say.

THE NATURE OF INTERNAL CUES

Edgar O'Neal's study advances hypotheses within the context of Mills' choice certainty theory (1968). In choice certainty theory, a person taking an action wants to be certain it is better than alternative actions. Certainty that an action is best is a function of the proportion of total cognitions favoring the action. An individual faced with a choice will attempt to increase his certainty regarding which action is best.

In a situation in which an individual is uncertain about a choice regarding other persons, he may attempt to increase certainty by changing cognitions about the other persons so that more cognitions favor the preferred persons and fewer cognitions favor the nonpreferred persons. Such behavior will increase the intercorrelation of traits attributed to the other persons.

O'Neal suggests that an individual who is uncertain

about a prospective choice will be aroused. If so, the individual is likely to interpret arousal as that accompanying uncertainty.

It follows, then, that if the individual is aroused by a drug (and is unaware of the exogenous origin of his arousal), his desire to increase his choice certainty will increase. With a greater desire to increase certainty, he may be expected to change more of his cognitions so that they support the favored alternative and do not support the nonfavored alternative. This should result in a greater intercorrelation of traits attributed to persons involved in his choice: a positive halo effect for preferred persons and a negative halo effect for the nonpreferred.

To recast O'Neal's experiment in terms of our analysis of Schachter's theory, caffeine triggers the internal cues associated with autonomic arousal, which stimulates evaluative needs and a process of explanation in which the subject makes use of cues in an anticipated choice. The explanation hypothetically adopted by the subject for his arousal is that he feels uncertain regarding the choice. The state of uncertainty leads to a desire to increase feelings of certainty. The increase is accomplished by changing cognitions about the stimulus persons, resulting in increased halo effects.

Thus, O'Neal gets from his experimental manipulation to his dependent variable by using Schachter's theory of emotion in tandem with Mills' choice certainty theory. The fact that his study obtains positive results increases our confidence in both theories.

The chapter by James Laird and Melvin Crosby, "Individual differences in self-attribution of emotion," clarifies our notion of what may constitute an internal cue. Schachter, working within the context of the James-Cannon controversy, spoke of internal cues as arising from a state of visceral arousal: a racing heart, sweaty hands, and so forth. Laird and Crosby's study consists in part of showing that when they place subjects' faces in a smiling position, the subjects feel happy; when they place their faces in a frowning position, the subjects feel sad. Thus, Laird and Crosby show that an internal cue may be kinesthetic as well as visceral.

But the study also shows that the nature of the internal cue may indicate the "direction" of the emotional state: if the kinesthetic cues indicate the face is in a smiling position, the emotion felt will be a happy one; if the cues indicate the face is in a frowning position, the emotion felt will be a sad one.

Laird and Crosby's study goes even further and shows that there are interesting individual differences in the extent to which a subject makes use of proprioceptive cues about the position of his face to infer what emotions he is feeling. Those who make extensive use of such cues experience emotional states in a manner similar to their experience of sensations; while those who do not, experience emotional states in a manner similar to their experience of making judgments.

Actually, it has been known for some time that an internal cue need not be the mere perception of visceral arousal. Externally supplied information about arousal state can function in the same way as perception of actual arousal, and the information need not even be directly about arousal, but simply information sufficient to cause the subject to make inferences about his arousal state.

Valins (1966), in what is by now a classic experiment, showed that cues about internal state need not derive from actual autonomic arousal, but might consist solely in the subject's belief that he was in a state of autonomic arousal. In Valins' study, subjects were shown pictures of *Playboy* nudes while listening to their supposed heart-rate (actually a recording of heart-like sounds). For half of the pictures, subjects heard their "heart-rate" change. These pictures were rated as more attractive than control pictures.

This volume includes an extension of this demonstration of the effects of externally-supplied information about internal state. In "Cognitive manipulation of GSR extinction: analogues for conditioning therapies," Koenig and Henriksen classically condition subjects so that they respond to the conditioned stimulus with a GSR. Koenig and Henriksen then show that conditioned GSRs extinguish more rapidly when subjects are informed that the unconditioned stimulus will not again be administered, than when subjects are not so informed. The finding that concerns us here, however, is that when subjects are informed that their galvanic-skin-responsiveness is high, GSR maintains itself at a higher level than when subjects are informed that their responsiveness is low. Thus the study both replicates Valins' demonstration concerning the effectiveness of externally supplied information about internal state and shows that such information actually affects physiological functioning.

In a study by Storms and Nisbett (1970), it was shown that information about internal state could be indirectly given to the subject. Insomniac subjects were given placebo pills to take a few minutes before going to bed. Some subjects were told that the pills would cause arousal (arousal condition) and others were told that the pills would reduce arousal (relaxation condition). It was found that arousal subjects got to sleep *more* quickly than they had on nights without the pills while relaxation subjects got to sleep *less* quickly than usual.

These results can be understood if we assume that the subjects go through a process of inference concerning both their experienced arousal level and their beliefs about whether it has been artificially increased or lowered. Presumably, the arousal subjects inferred that their "own" arousal was low, since the experienced arousal was about average for them, yet it was being enhanced by a pill. Similarly, relaxation subjects must have assumed that their "own" arousal was unusually intense since their experienced arousal level was about average even after taking an arousal-reducing agent.

The study by London and Monello, "Cognitive manipulation of boredom," goes even further in broadening the notion of what an internal cue may be. The cue is neither autonomic nor kinesthetic. In the London-Monello study, subjects are set to performing a task. A rigged clock leads subjects to believe that the task, actually lasting twenty physical minutes, lasted either ten minutes or thirty minutes. It was predicted that subjects in the "ten minute" condition would become more bored by the task, given that, from the subjects' point of view, time passed more slowly in that condition than in the "thirty minute" condition. Subjects in the London-Monello study, then, are put in the position of trying to explain to themselves why time is passing slowly or quickly. That is, the internal cue is the feeling that time is passing at a rate different than usual. These differences in inferred internal state result in differences in reported emotional state.

EVALUATIVE NEEDS

In Brendan Maher's chapter, "Delusional thinking and cognitive disorder," our attention is directed to the evaluative needs aroused by internal cues. Maher outlines the evidence that a group of psychiatric patients--acute schizophrenics--suffer from "primary perceptual anomalies". These anomalies, suggests Maher, demand explanation in precisely the same way that autonomic arousal in Schachter's experiments demands explanation. Given the striking nature of the perceptual experience arising from these biological anomalies, the patient turns to dramatic explanations. These explanations seem bizarre to observers, who do not have access to the experience of the patient, and the patient is labeled as schizophrenic.

Maher's theory of the development of delusions suggests a form of treatment. Maher proposes that the patient be informed that he is having perceptual experiences unlike those of others because of a biological anomaly. The patient would be told, in effect, that just as some people have defective hearts or gall bladders, he has a defective reticular activating system. Thus, the patient might be prevented from adopting "crazy" explanations for his unusual experiences and in this way a delusional system will be avoided.

THE PROCESS OF EXPLAINING INTERNAL CUES

With Barefoot and Straub's chapter, "Opportunity for information search and the effect of false heart rate feedback," we move on to consideration of another step in Schachter's theory, the process of explanation. Barefoot and Straub carried out an extension of Valins' (1966) phenomenon (which we have already mentioned), that subjects given false feedback about their heart rate while viewing pictures of nudes find those nudes more attractive than nudes viewed without false feedback. Barefoot and Straub suggest, following Valins, that the subject given false feedback searches the slides for features of the nude which might have caused the reaction in his heart rate. "In effect," propose Barefoot and Straub, "the subject convinced himself that the slide was attractive, and he invested considerable cognitive effort in this self-persuasion process."

Since this hypothetical process of self-persuasion requires a certain amount of time for searching the slides, Barefoot and Straub can put the postulated process to direct test. They show that the Valins effect obtains only when subjects are given a considerable length of time to examine the pictures in light of the false feedback; the effect does not obtain when subjects are not given ample time. Their finding supports Valins' notion that the process of explanation is an active process, that it involves cognitive work, that it is more like hypothesis-testing than like Schachter's (1971) notion of a passive labeling.

Valins' study, "Persistent effects of information about internal reactions: ineffectiveness of debriefing," makes a point quite similar to Barefoot and Straub's. Subjects in this experiment were shown slides of female nudes while supposedly hearing their heart-rate reactions. They were subsequently informed that these reactions were part of a deception. Valins notes that, although subjects accepted the debriefing, the false information continued to exert an influence on their attitudes toward the nudes. These attitudes were the same as the attitudes of subjects who were not debriefed. It seems that once subjects have gone through the process of explaining their internal cues, that explanation and its consequent emotion are not lightly set aside, not even by the information that the original "internal cue" which stimulated the process was phony. Like Barefoot and Straub's chapter, Valins' chapter suggests that the subject has worked to explain the internal cue so that the explanation arrived at is not easily displaced.

THE EFFECTS OF EXTERNAL CUES

Five chapters in this volume speak to the issue of the external cue in terms of which, according to Schachter's theory, people seek to explain their puzzling internal states.

Aaron Beck's chapter, "Cognition, affect, and psychopathology," fits neatly within Schachter's framework. Schachter has always claimed that a chief advantage of his theory is that it takes the burden of explaining the great variety of experienced emotions off physiology (where the burden had been placed by James' (1890) theory of emotion), and places that burden on the variety of external cues with which we come in contact.

Viewed in these terms, Beck spells out four formulae (external cues) which can lead to emotional states or, under some conditions, to psychopathological conditions. Thus, if the stimulus situation can be summarized by the formula "I have lost x," the feeling engendered will be either one of sadness or under more extreme conditions, depression. "I have gained x" will lead either to the feeling of euphoria or, if idiosyncratically conceptualized, hypomania. If the situation can be summarized by "x is dangerous," then the feeling of anxiety will be engendered or, more extremely, an anxiety neurosis will be triggered. Finally, if the situation falls within the rubric "x has offended me," then either the feeling of anger will be engendered or, under certain conditions, the state of paranoia. Beck's chapter is valuable insofar as it spells out general cognitive formulae, each of which captures a variety of concrete situations. It also postulates a series of continua which link ordinary emotions to states of psychopathology.

The chapter by Spanos, Barber and Lang, "Cognition and self-control: cognitive control of painful sensory input," describes a study in which, among other things, subjects were first tested for base-level response to a pain-producing stimulus and then were re-tested on the same pain stimulus after receiving an experimental treatment. Experimental condition subjects were given "instructions for anesthesia:" "think of the hand as numb and insensitive as if it were a piece of rubber..." Control subjects were given no such instructions. The anesthesia instructions produced a reduction in pain compared to the control condition.

The study, like Beck's, is relevant to step IV in Schachter's theory. In the Spanos et al. study, however, unlike Schachter's theory, the person need not search for an explanation of a puzzling internal cue and does not himself come to an explanation in terms of an external cue. Rather, the subject is, in effect, handed an external cue by the experimenter who says "here, think this way."

Parenthetically, it might be mentioned that an equally important thrust of the Spanos et al. chapter is its point in regard to hypnosis. In addition to the anesthesia variable, Spanos, Barber and Lang manipulate the presence/absence of an hypnotic induction. Spanos, Barber and Lang thus separate instructions calculated to reduce pain from instructions to enter hypnosis and show that while hypnosis *per se* does not reduce pain, instructions specifically aimed at pain reduction do have such an effect.

"Self-Persuasion and Fear Reduction from Escape Behavior" by Klemp and Leventhal makes an additional point about the nature of the external cue. The chapter marks overlapping conceptual frameworks of Stanley Schachter and Daryl Bem. Bem (1967, 1972) has labored to show that an individual may use his own behavior as data from which to infer his beliefs. Putting this in terms of Schachter's theory of emotion, an individual may use his own behavior as an external cue to explain his internal state.

In the original study drawn upon by Klemp and Leventhal (Bandler, Madaras, and Bem, 1968), conditions were set up so that it appeared to subjects that they were spontaneously choosing either to (a) turn off (i.e., escape from) a shock or (b) not turn off (i.e., sustain) a shock. When subjects believed that they chose to escape from the shock they rated the shock as significantly more painful than when they believed that they chose to sustain the shock. Thus, a subject used his own behavior (escaping vs. sustaining) as an element in his interpretation of his internal state (the shock hurt more vs. less).

The Klemp and Leventhal chapter makes the important point that there are marked individual differences in the Bandler et al. phenomenon. In their experiment, Klemp and Leventhal found that the effect obtains only when the subject has a high degree of tolerance for shock. The experimenters argue for the plausibility of such a finding. Low tolerance subjects are fearful and are likely to be more responsive to the shock than to the inferences to be drawn from their behavior, while high tolerance subjects are quite the opposite: for them, their behavior in the situation is likely to be more salient than the shock.

Subjects in "perceived anger level, instigating

agent, and aggression," an experiment carried out by Berkowitz and Turner, were provoked by a confederate and were then exposed to two experimental variables in a factorial design.

Subjects were led to believe they felt varying degrees of anger towards the confederate. This was accomplished by means of an "anger meter" which supposedly integrated several aspects of the subject's physiological state. This manipulation, although superficially similar to Valins' false heart-rate manipulation, is really quite different. In Valins' study, subjects took the false feedback as physiological data and made their own inferences concerning its meaning for their emotional state. Berkowitz and Turner's feedback is a blunt, externally-supplied description of the subject's emotional state.

The second variable in the Berkowitz and Turner study was the requirement to give shocks (under an appropriate ruse) either to their provoker or to a neutral confederate. As predicted, Berkowitz and Turner found a systematic relationship between the anger feedback and shock delivered by subjects in the "provoker" condition, and none in the neutral target condition. The investigators take this finding to mean that they have gone a step beyond Schachter's theory insofar as they have predicted behavior (giving shocks) consequent upon an emotional state (anger).

At most, Berkowitz and Turner do extend Schachter's theory; at least, they make explicit what has been implicit in Schachter's work. In certain of his studies of emotion, Schachter has measured behavior (as distinguished from a self-report of emotional state) but Schachter has conceived of that measurement, not precisely as a measure of behavior which the emotion causes (a la Berkowitz and Turner), but simply as a measure of the emotional state itself.

We turn lastly to the chapter by Nisbett and Storms, "Cognitive and social determinants of food intake".

Schachter's initial approach to the study of obesity was to view it as the result of both oversusceptibility to external cues (taste, the conviviality of the meal setting, etc.) and undersusceptibility to internal cues (gut motility, etc.). The approach led directly out of his work on emotion, and was essentially a direct application of the internal/external paradigm to the motivational state of hunger.

Three experiments are reported by Nisbett and Storms, all of which tested the hypothesis that the food intake of overweight individuals is more affected by external cues of a cognitive or social nature than is the food intake of individuals who are not overweight. All of the experiments indicate that the food intake of people *in general* is affected by cognitive and social cues, but none of them indicate that overweight individuals are more responsive to such cues than other individuals.

The Nisbett-Storms experiments thus suggest a redefinition of the external cues triggering eating, at least with regard to obese susceptibility to such cues. The obese have been shown elsewhere to be overly susceptible to a variety of sensory cues: taste, sight, proximity, etc. Nisbett and Storms have shown that the obese are probably not overly susceptible to non-sensory external cues. This fact throws into question the original application of the emotions paradigm to hunger while simultaneously demonstrating its utility in generating productive research questions in this area.

The studies in this volume, then, speak to a wide range of issues in the field of motivation and emotion. They share common bonds of inspiration by, relevance to, and sometimes criticism of, the original formulation of emotion in terms of external vs. internal cues proposed by Schachter and Singer in 1962.

REFERENCES

Bandler, R.J., Madaras, G.R., and Bem, D.J. 1968. Self-observation as a source of pain perception. *Journal of Personality and Social Psychology* 9:205-209.

Bem, D.J. 1967. Self-perception: An alternative interpretation of cognitive dissonance phenomena. *Psychological Review* 74:183-200.

------. 1972. Self-perception theory. *In* L. Berkowitz (ed.), *Advances in Experimental Social Psychology*, Vol. 6. New York: Academic Press.

James, W. 1890. *The Principles of Psychology*. New York: Henry Holt.

Mills, J. 1968. Interest in supporting and discrepant

information. *In* R. Abelson et al., *Theories of Cognitive Consistency: A Sourcebook*. Chicago: Rand McNally.

Schachter, S. 1964. The interaction of cognitive and physiological determinants of emotional state. *In* L. Berkowitz (ed.), *Advances in Experimental Social Psychology*, Vol. I. New York: Academic Press.

----. 1971. *Emotion, Obesity, and Crime*. New York: Academic Press.

Schachter, S., and Singer, J. 1962. Cognitive, Social, and physiological determinants of emotional state. *Physiological Review* 69:379-399.

Storms, M., and Nisbett, R. 1970. Insomnia and the attribution process. *Journal of Personality and Social Psychology* 16:319-328.

Valins, S. 1966. Cognitive effects of false heart rate feedback. *Journal of Personality and Social Psychology* 4:400-408.

II

The Nature of Internal Cues

3

Edgar O'Neal

Influence of Future Choice Importance and Arousal Upon the Halo Effect

Two determinants of the magnitude of the influence of anticipated choice on the halo effect are investigated: importance of future choice and arousal. Male subjects ranked photographs on positive personality traits. Half of the photographs were of persons about which they anticipated making a choice. In confirmation of the hypotheses, (a) the intercorrelation of the rankings was greater for the choice photographs than for the nonchoice photographs when the subjects anticipated an important choice, but not when they anticipated an unimportant choice; and (b) the intercorrelation was greater for the choice photographs than for the nonchoice photographs when the subjects were aroused by caffeine and uninformed as to the source of their arousal, but not when they were informed as to the source of their arousal or not aroused.

This study[1] was designed to investigate two possible determinants of the halo effect[2]: the importance of future choice and arousal. The hypotheses were advanced within the context of choice certainty proposed by Mills (1968).

Reprinted from the *Journal of Personality and Social Psychology*, 1971, Vol. 19, No. 3, 334-340.

According to choice certainty theory, before a person takes an action, he wants to be certain that it is better than the alternative actions. The theory assumes that certainty that an action is best will be a function of the proportion of total cognitions favoring that action; the higher the proportion, the greater the certainty. An individual faced with a choice will attempt to increase his certainty regarding which action is best and will avoid decreasing his certainty. This theory is similar to Jones and Gerard's (1967) conceptualization of the unequivocal behavioral orientation. It differs from Janis' (Mann, Janis, and Chaplin, 1969) conflict position, since it does not invoke anticipation of postdecisional regret as motivational construct.

In a recent study, the influence of future choice upon the halo effect was investigated (O'Neal and Mills, 1969). It was reasoned that persons uncertain about a future choice regarding other persons may attempt to increase their certainty by changing their cognitions about the other persons so that (a) more of them favor the preferred persons and (b) fewer of them favor the nonpreferred persons. The effect of this should be to increase the intercorrelation of the traits att ibuted to the other persons. In the O'Neal and Mills study, male college students ranked female photographs of two different sizes on a number of desirable traits after they had been told that half of the photographs of each size were of promiscuous girls and that in a later experiment they would choose among the photographs of one size (the choice set) which were the promiscuous girls. It was expected that choice photo rankings would be more highly intercorrelated than the rankings of the other photographs because there would be a greater tendency for subjects to rank uniformly high those choice photos they favor and as uniformly low those choice photos they do not favor. As predicted, the intercorrelation of the ranking of the photographs in the choice set was higher than the intercorrelation of rankings of the other photographs.

The first purpose of the present study was to determine the influence of the importance of an anticipated choice upon the halo effect. Although not explicitly stated in choice certainty theory (Mills, 1968), it seems reasonable that if a person anticipates making a choice and is uncertain, the more important the choice, the greater the desire to achieve certainty. The consequences of an unfavorable outcome would be more severe in the case of a more important anticipated choice, and so the desire to be certain about the choice should be greater.

With a greater desire for certainty, an individual anticipating an important choice about which he is uncertain could be expected to change even more of his cognitions so that they support the favored alternative and do not support the nonfavored alternative. This should produce a still greater tendency toward the halo effect for the individual anticipating an important choice involving other persons. The first hypothesis of the present study was as follows: The anticipation of making important choices about other persons will produce a greater tendency toward the halo effect than will the anticipation of making unimportant choices about other persons.

The second purpose of the study involved the influence of physiological arousal and anticipated choice upon the halo effect. To be sure, the concept of arousal is not an entirely clear one. Early theorists (e.g., Malmo, 1958) tended to view arousal as a unitary concept, hence the ubiquitous term "general" arousal. But some recent critics (Lacey, 1967; Routtenberg, 1968; Taylor and Epstein, 1967) presented evidence that general arousal is produced by the activity of a number of physiological subsystems. Despite these recent criticisms, it still seems to make sense to speak of arousal in a general sense, since the proposed subsystems are usually correlated (Lacey, 1967). For the present purpose, therefore, no attempt was made to distinguish among possible subsystems producing arousal.

Recent research in cognitive dissonance suggests that arousal might accompany lack of certainty regarding a choice. Although choice certainty theory differs from dissonance theory, in that it deals with behavior prior to commitment, and dissonance theory does not (Festinger, 1957, 1964), both make predictions of changes in cognitive organization. Gerard (1964) argued that cognitive dissonance affects arousal. Buckhout (1966) recorded heart rate data while subjects were verbally reinforced for choosing to read aloud statements opposite to their initial attitude. Buckhout reported that subjects whose attitude change was in the direction of the reinforced position showed a higher degree of initial heart rate increase and a greater subsequent decrease than did subjects whose attitude change was not in the reinforced direction.

In a study more directly related to arousal prior to choice, Berlyne (1961, Experiment II) read words to subjects and asked the subjects to respond with the first word that came to mind. The stimulus words had previously been rated by Laffal (1955) for their response uncertainty (entropy, H) value: those that evoked a wide variety of free association responses were rated high in response uncertainty, and those which produced a narrower range of responses were rated low in response uncertainty. Berlyne found that subjects' galvanic skin response amplitude was greater following presentation of words high in response uncertainty value than words low in response uncertainty value.

Mann et al. (1969) had subjects choose between two unpleasant physiological stimulations and reported that prior to announcing their choice, the subjects' heart rates increased. However, the heart rate increase could have been due simply to anticipation of the unpleasant stimuli. Despite this reservation regarding the results of this latter study, it does not seem unreasonable to posit that an individual who is uncertain about a prospective choice will be aroused; and moreover, that the less certainty the individual has about his anticipated choice, the more his arousal.

If it is true that lack of certainty about an anticipated choice is accompanied by arousal, then when an individual is aroused, under certain conditions he may interpret his arousal as that accompanying lack of certainty. Providing that the arousal occurs in a situation similar to those in the past in which the individual experienced lack of certainty, he may use his level of arousal as an indication of the degree of his lack of certainty. If the individual were aroused for another reason--say, from a cup of coffee--then an anticipated choice provides cues that he may use to attribute his arousal to that ordinarily accompanying lack of certainty. However, this should not occur if the individual were aware that a portion of his arousal was due to another source, because he could "discount" a portion of his arousal as being not due to lack of certainty (cf. Nisbett and Schachter, 1966).

It would seem to follow from this line of reasoning that if he is not aware of the source of his arousal, the more aroused the individual who is uncertain about an anticipated choice, the greater will be his desire to increase his certainty. With a greater desire to increase certainty, he might therefore be expected to change more of his cognitions so that they support the favored alternative and do not support the nonfavored alternative, than if he were either less aroused or able to discount a portion of the arousal. This should result in a greater intercorrelation of the traits that he attributes to persons involved in his anticipated choice. The second hypothesis, therefore, was as follows: The anticipation of making choices about other persons will produce a greater tendency toward the halo effect when the individual is more highly aroused and unaware that a portion of his arousal is from a source other than lack of certainty.

METHOD

Overview

Under the guise of a "space-flight drug study," male subjects were told that they would later have to choose from among eight photographs the photographs of four men they would most like to work with in a group task. Then they ranked these photographs (choice photos) and eight other (control) photos on a number of positive attributes.

Ten subjects were randomly assigned to each of six experimental conditions: aroused-misinformed, high importance; aroused-misinformed, low importance; aroused-informed, high importance; aroused-informed, low importance; not aroused, high importance; and not aroused, low importance. In the high-importance conditions, the subjects were told that their choice would definitely determine who their partners would be in the group task; and, in the low-importance conditions, the subjects were told that there was only a small chance that it would determine who their partners would be. In the aroused-misinformed conditions, the subjects were given caffeine and told that they had received a vitamin; in the aroused-informed conditions, they were given caffeine and told that it was a stimulant; and, in the not-aroused conditions, they were given a placebo and were told that it was a vitamin. For half of the subjects in each condition, the choice photos were one set of eight photographs; and for half of the subjects in each condition, the choice photos were the other set of eight photographs.

Procedure

Male undergraduates in introductory psychology were screened by a telephone interview to exclude as subjects those students with contraindications for caffeine. In the telephone interview, the experimenter introduced himself as a researcher conducting a space-flight drug study, who had been given the student's name and telephone number by a member of the psychology department. The student was asked if he was willing to participate in both of two 50-minute sessions and if had any objections to taking drugs. Two students who were contacted refused to participate because the study involved the use of drugs. The remainder were asked a number of questions, some intended to disguise the true nature of the experiment, and others intended to identify students for whom taking caffeine would be detrimental to their health. Twelve prospective subjects were excluded because they indicated that they had suffered from either heart, kidney, or stomach ailments. Appointments were made with the others, and they were directed to the experimental room, in the University of Missouri Student Health Center.[3]

At the experimental room, the experimenter introduced himself and stated that the purpose of the experiment was concerned with the effect of certain drugs upon the group performance of standard space-flight tasks: during the first session some base-line recordings would be made of the subject's physiological reactions to a drug, and at the second session the subject would be given the same drug and would work on some space-flight problems with four other undergraduates.

The subject's pulse was taken at the wrist for a

full-minute interval by the male experimenter. Then the subject was asked to read a description of the effects of four drugs identified by the letters A, B, C, and D and to sign a statement indicating his consent to take one dose of one of them. Drug A was described as a vitamin that might result in slightly increased appetite and thirst. Drug B was described as a stimulant that might result in slightly increased heart rate. The drug-description sheet included a statement that experimental considerations might not permit informing the subject as to which one of the four drugs he would be given.

The subject was seated at a table on which were four bottles labeled "Drug A," "Drug B," etc., corresponding to the letter designations of the drugs on the drug-effect sheet the subject had read. Each of the bottles contained either caffeine in size #00 capsules or milk sugar placebo capsules of the same size. The caffeine capsules contained 200 milligrams of caffeine (the amount in 1-1/2 - 2 cups of coffee) obtained by crushing two tablets of NoDoz (Grove Laboratories Division of Bristol-Myers), plus lactose. NoDoz is available without prescription, and the dosage of 200 milligrams is a therapeutic amount recommended on the box for adults.

Before giving the subject the capsule, the experimenter mentioned that the drug received would be the stimulant/vitamin and asked if the subject had read the effects of the stimulant/vitamin on the sheet. Depending upon the condition to which the subject had been assigned, the experimenter took out a bottle labeled either "stimulant" or "vitamin" and gave the subject either the caffeine or placebo capsule. Just before giving the subject the capsule, the experimenter said again that the drug he had been assigned to take was the stimulant/vitamin.

Then the subject was told that it would take 30 minutes for the drug to take effect and that the experimenter would return in a few minutes. At this point the experimenter left the room for 12 minutes. Upon returning, the experimenter introduced the anticipated choice by stating that a second purpose of the study was to investigate the effect of crew congeniality upon the success of space flights. It was explained to the subject that one way to maximize the chance of congeniality might be to allow the captain of a mission to select his crew members. The experimenter went on to say that in order to simulate such a selection process, he was using photographs of all participants in the study and that he would take a Polaroid snapshot of the subject before the conclusion of the day's session.

Each subject was told that later he would choose the photographs of the four men with whom he would most like to work in the second session. The experimenter told each subject in the *high-importance* condition that he had been randomly designated captain and that his choices would therefore determine the makeup of his space-flight group in the second session. It was explained to each subject in the *low-importance* condition that there was only a small chance--about 1 in 10--of his randomly being designated captain and therefore little likelihood of his choice actually determining the make-up of his space-flight group.

The experimenter provided the subject with a rationale for the ranking task by saying that there was need for a check on the influence of first-impression factors in the space-flight group's success, and that the check would involve the subject's ranking photos of the other participants--those currently participating and those who participated last semester--according to a number of personality traits. It was explained to the subject that he would first rank the photographs and then choose the photographs of the four men with whom he would most like to work.

Then the experimenter arranged the 16 photos of male students at another university in a uniform order in front of the subject. The 8 control photos each had a small slip of paper attached marked "assigned." After the photographs were displayed for the subject, the experimenter said:

> You'll notice that some of the photos are tagged, and some are not. The tagged ones--let's see, there are eight of them--are of men who participated in the study last semester. The photos without tags are of current participants, and it is from among these that you will later select four as being of men you would like to work with next time.

As a check on the effects of the arousal manipulation, the pulse rate was taken for a second time. At this point approximately 30 minutes had elapsed since administration of the capsule. The experimenter's excuse for taking pulse rate again was that he had neglected to write down the pulse rate earlier and that he had forgotten what it was.

The subject then ranked the 16 photographs on each of eight traits: considerate, energetic, fearless, patient, resourceful, responsible, sincere, and studious. At the completion of the rankings, the experimenter mentioned to the subject that there was something about the experiment that he had not told him and asked the subject what he thought it could be. None of the subjects' responses indicated that they had been aware of the true purpose of the experiment. Finally, the experimenter revealed the true nature of the experiment to the subject, including the name, dosage, and effects of the drug he had taken, and asked him not to discuss the experiment with anyone.

RESULTS

Effectiveness of the Arousal Manipulation

Before considering the effects of the experimental conditions upon the dependent variable, it is appropriate to present the results of a check on the manipulation of arousal.[4] The mean change in pulse rate in beats per minute for subjects in each condition, from prior to administration of the capsule to approximately 20 minutes after administering the capsule, is presented in Table 3.1. Positive values in the table represent an increase in mean pulse, and negative values, a decrease.

It may be noted that there was an increase in mean pulse rate for the subjects in the four aroused conditions and a decrease for the subjects in the two not-aroused conditions. This latter decrease may have been due to the fact that the pulse rate was elevated initially as a result of climbing the two flights of stairs to the experimental room, and subsequently depressed by a few minutes of rest.

TABLE 3.1. Mean Pulse Rate Change (In Beats Per Minute)

Importance	*Arousal*			
	Aroused-misinformed	*Aroused-informed*	*Not aroused*	*Total*
High	6.2_a	6.9_a	-2.9_b	3.4
Low	6.7_a	3.5_a	-3.2_b	2.3
Total	6.5	5.2	-3.1	

Note: -n=10. Cells not having a subscript in common are significantly different at the .05 level by the Duncan multiple-range test.

An analysis of variance of the mean change in pulse rate yielded a highly significant effect $F=21.58$, $df=2/54$, $p<.001$) for the arousal factor. There were no differences in mean pulse rate change significant at the .05 level by the Duncan multiple-range test among individual cells in the aroused conditions or between the two cells in the not-aroused conditions. However, each cell in the aroused conditions differed significantly ($p<.05$) from each cell in the not-aroused conditions. It would appear from these data that caffeine had the effect of increasing physiological arousal. Moreover, the data indicate that this occurred regardless of whether the subjects were informed or misinformed about the source of their caffeine-induced arousal.

Effects of the Importance of Anticipated Choice

Each subject's ranking of the photographs on each trait was converted into two revised rankings, one for the choice photos and one for the control photos. These revised rankings are based on the order, within its set, of the subject's ranking of each photograph. This conversion yielded a 1-8 ranking for the choice photos and a 1-8 ranking for the control photos on each of the traits. Coefficients of concordance, Kendall's *W*, were computed for the revised rankings of the choice photos (choice *W*) and also for the revised rankings of the control photos (control *W*). Kendall's *W* bears a linear relationship to the average Spearman rank-order correlation

TABLE 3.2. Means of the Coefficients of Concordance (*W*)

Importance	*Choice-no choice*	*Arousal*			
		Aroused-misinformed	*Aroused-informed*	*Not Aroused*	*Total*
	Choice	.54	.48	.42	.48
High	Control	.27	.41	.36	.35
	Choice minus control	.26	.07	.06	.13
	Choice	.50	.43	.33	.42
Low	Control	.33	.43	.41	.39
	Choice minus control	.16	.00	-.07	.03
	Choice	.52	.45	.38	.45
Total	Control	.30	.42	.38	.37
	Choice minus control	.21	.03	-.01	.08

Note: -n=10.

between all possible pairs of the rankings. The means of the coefficients of concordance are presented in Table 3.2.

According to the first hypothesis, the anticipation of making important choices about other persons will produce a greater tendency toward the halo effect than will the anticipation of making unimportant choices about other persons. It was expected from the first hypothesis that the choice *W* should exceed the control *W* by a larger margin in the high-importance conditions than in the low-importance conditions. The choice *W* minus control *W* differences are presented in Table 3.2. It will be noted that this difference is greater for those subjects in the high-importance conditions (.13) than for those in the low-importance conditions (.03).

A repeated-measures analysis of variance (Table 3.3) yielded significance for the Importance x Choice - No Choice interaction ($F = 7.61$, $df = 1/54$, $p < .01$). According to prediction, the choice *W* minus control *W* differences are significantly greater in the high-importance conditions than in the low-importance conditions. The results of this test lend strong support to the first hypothesis. Subjects who anticipated an important choice regarding other persons demonstrated a greater tendency toward the halo effect in the traits attributed to these other persons than did subjects who anticipated an unimportant choice regarding the other persons.

Effects of Arousal

The second hypothesis stated that the anticipation of making choices about other persons would produce a greater tendency toward the halo effect when the individual is more highly aroused and unaware that a portion of his arousal is from a source other than lack of certainty. From this second hypothesis it would be expected that the choice *W* minus control *W* difference should be greater in the aroused-misinformed conditions than in either the aroused-informed or not-aroused conditions. A potential obstacle to the interpretation of the choice *W* minus control *W* differences would exist if there were differences among the conditions in control *W*. Indeed, the control *W* appears (see Table 3.2) to be lowest in the aroused-misinformed conditions. However,

TABLE 3.3. Summary of Repeated-Measures Analysis of Variance of Means of Coefficients of Concordance *(W)*

Source	*df*	*MS*	*F*
Between	59		
Importance (A)	1	9.64	.09
Arousal (B)	2	86.48	.79
A X B	2	9.28	.08
Error	54	109.31	
Within	60		
Choice-no choice (C)	1	524.82	18.22*
A X C	1	219.01	7.61*
B X C	2	364.34	12.65*
A X B X C	2	6.84	.24
Error	54	28.79	

*$p < .01$.

an analysis of variance of the control *W*s revealed that the effects of the arousal factor upon control *W*s is not significant ($F = 2.55$, $df = 2/54$). Therefore, there appears to be no compelling reason why the choice *W* minus control *W* differences could not provide evidence for the second hypothesis.

The arousal factor produced significant effects upon the choice *W* minus control *W* differences, these effects being evident in the significant Arousal X Choice - No Choice interaction ($F = 12.65$, $df = 1/54$, $p < .01$) in the repeated-measures analysis of variance (Table 3.3). Comparisons were made of the difference among the three levels of the arousal factor in the choice *W* minus control *W* difference. The difference between the aroused-misinformed conditions and the aroused-informed conditions was significant beyond the .01 level ($t = 3.47$, $df = 38$). Also, the difference between the aroused-misinformed and unaroused levels reached the same significance ($t = 3.62$, $df = 38$, $p < .01$). No significance was obtained for the difference between the aroused-informed and the not-aroused levels of the arousal factor. In confirmation of the second hypothesis, arousal increased the influence of choice on the halo effect when the person aroused was unaware of the source of his artificially induced arousal.

DISCUSSION

While the results strongly support the two hypotheses, one other aspect of the data deserves consideration. Although not explicitly hypothesized in the present study, it would be expected that the rankings of the photographs involved in the future choice would be more highly intercorrelated than the rankings of the other photos, that is, that the choice *W* would exceed the control *W* for the subjects in all conditions. This outcome would seem to be in harmony with those results reported by O'Neal and Mills (1969).

The significant main effect obtained for the choice-no choice factor in the analysis of variance (Table 3.3) does not permit an unqualified conclusion, however, because of the interactions between choice-no choice and arousal, and choice-no choice and importance. The choice *W* was significantly greater than the control *W* only in the two aroused-misinformed conditions and in the aroused-informed, high-importance conditions. The evidence indicates that anticipated choice increases the halo effect only when the choice is important and the individual is aroused.

This result is not necessarily in conflict with the O'Neal and Mills (1969) results. They reported a higher intercorrelation in the rankings of choice photos by male subjects who anticipated choosing which photos were of "promiscuous girls." It can plausibly be argued that the situation confronted by the subjects in the O'Neal and Mills study resembles most closely that faced by the subjects in the aroused, high-importance conditions in the present experiment. Choices regarding photographs of promiscuous girls could well have produced arousal. Also, choices regarding the promiscuity of females would seem to be at least as important for male subjects as a choice of preferred partners in a group task. The results of the present study replicate the study by O'Neal and Mills if it is assumed that the choice in the earlier study was important and that the subjects were somewhat aroused.

The results, together with the foregoing explanation of the situation faced by subjects in the O'Neal and Mills (1969) study, make possible tentative conclusions about two assumptions implicit in choice certainty. It would seem that the predicted effects of lack of certainty regarding an anticipated choice occur only if the choice is a fairly important one. While it is not possible to say precisely how important an anticipated choice must be before the effects of lack of certainty are produced, it seems clear that lack of certainty regarding a trivial choice (perhaps such as the one faced by the subjects in the low-importance condition) does not produce them. Finally, it would appear that arousal is an important component of the motivation to increase certainty regarding an anticipated choice.

NOTES

1. This study was conducted during the tenure of a National Institutes of Health Predoctoral Research Fellowship and was facilitated by a grant from the National Science Foundation to the University of Missouri, Judson Mills, principal investigator. Thanks are due to Judson Mills for advice and suggestions and to Russell Geen and Jefferson L. Sulzer for comments on an earlier version. Requests for reprints should be sent to the author, Department of Psychology, Newcomb College, Tulane University, New Orleans, Louisiana 70118.

2. The halo effect is defined by Jones and Gerard (1967:713) as "The tendency for trait ratings to show a higher intercorrelation than would be revealed by more objective measurement."

3. Appreciation must be expressed to William R. Galeota, Director of Student Health Services and Professor of Psychology at the University of Missouri, who supervised the administration of caffeine and provided research space in the Student Health Center.

4. There were no significant differences by analysis of variance among the conditions in initial pulse rate. The mean initial pulse rates, in beats per minute, were as follows: high importance-misinformed, 76.9; high importance-informed, 77.4; high importance-not aroused, 78.1; low importance-misinformed, 77.3; low importance-informed, 78.3; low importance-not aroused, 77.5.

REFERENCES

Berlyne, D. 1961. Conflict and the orientation reaction. *Journal of Experimental Psychology* 62:476-483.

Buckhout, R. 1966. Changes in heart rate accompanying attitude change. *Journal of Personality and Social Psychology* 4:695-699.

Festinger, L. 1957. *A theory of cognitive dissonance*. Stanford: Stanford University Press.

Festinger, L. 1964. *Conflict, decision, and dissonance*. Stanford: Stanford University Press.

Gerard, H. 1964. Physiological measurement in social psychological research. *In* P. Leiderman and D. Shapiro (eds.), *Psychobiological approaches to social behavior*. Stanford: Stanford University Press.

Jones, E. and Gerard, H. 1967. *Foundations of social psychology*. New York: Wiley.

Lacey, J. 1967. Somatic response patterning and stress: Some revisions of activation theory. *In* M. Appley and R. Trumbull (eds.), *Psychological stress*. New York: Appleton.

Laffal, J. 1955. Response faults in word association as a function of response entropy. *Journal of Abnormal and Social Psychology* 50:265-270.

Malmo, R. 1958. Measurement of drive: An unsolved problem in psychology. *Nebraska Symposium on Motivation* 6:229-265.

Mann, L., Janis, I., and Chaplin, R. 1969. Effects of anticipation of forthcoming information on predecisional processes. *Journal of Personality and Social Psychology* 11:10-16.

Mills, J. 1968. Interest in supporting and discrepant information. *In* R. Abelson et al., *Theories of cognitive consistency: A sourcebook*. Chicago: Rand McNally.

Nisbett, R., and Schachter, S. 1966. Cognitive manipulation of pain. *Journal of Experimental Social Psychology* 2:227-236.

O'Neal, E., and Mills, J. 1969. The influence of anticipated choice on the halo effect. *Journal of Experimental Social Psychology* 5:347-351.

Routtenberg, A. 1968. The two-arousal hypothesis: Reticular formation and limbic system. *Psychological Review* 75:51-80.

Taylor, S., and Epstein, S. 1967. The measurement of autonomic arousal. *Psychosomatic Medicine* 29:514-525.

4

James Laird and
Melvin Crosby

Individual Differences in Self-Attribution of Emotion

Previous research demonstrating self-attribution phenomena has generally involved manipulation of S's behavior and subsequent measurement of self-attribution from this behavior. In addition to these "self-produced cues," it is suggested that people use "situational cues," and that individuals differ in the relative importance of these two kinds of cues in inferring attributes. In each of two replications, expressive behavior of 26 Ss was manipulated without their awareness, and changes in emotional experience measured. Ss' emotional response or lack of response to the manipulation of expression was consistent between replications. Ss who responded to the manipulation of expression also differed from non-responders in their reports about everyday emotional experience. These results were interpreted as supporting the hypothesis that, at least with respect to the attribution of emotional experience, people differ in the importance of self-produced cues.

How does an individual come to "know" what his own attitudes, motives, abilities and emotions are? A variety of recent studies have all seemed to suggest the same answer. In each case the answer has been that an individual may come to know his own attributes in the same way that he comes to know the attributes of others; by inference from the behavior that expresses these attributes.

The largest program of research related to this position arises out of Festinger's (1957) study of cognitive dissonance. As Bem (1967) has pointed out, probably all dissonance research can be interpreted within the self-inference paradigm. For example, in the classical forced-compliance situations (e.g., Festinger and Carlsmith, 1959), *S*s may be seen as inferring their attitudes from their statements about their attitudes. A very different kind of behavior was manipulated by Schachter and his associates (Schachter and Singer, (1962), who manipulated level of physiological arousal via injections of adrenalin. The group injected with adrenalin and unaware of what its effects would be experienced much more intense emotions than did an appropriate control group. Thus it appeared that *S*s attributed their heightened arousal to their emotion, and hence "felt" the emotion as more intense.

In a procedure, analogous to Schachter's, Laird (1967, in press) manipulated another aspect of emotional behavior. Under the guise of obtaining electrophysiological recordings of facial muscles under tension, *S*s were induced to frown or smile. Smiling *S*s reported feeling more elated than frowning *S*s. These various studies make it reasonable to assert that an individual's conception of himself and his properties may be formed through observation and interpretation of his own behavior.

However, in discussions of self-attribution, another possible data source for self-inference seems to have been overlooked. When we infer the attributes of another person, we make use not only of his behavior, but of his situation. If, for instance, we know a man has been insulted, we need no information about his behavior to infer that he is offended or angry, because "most people would be." If he is at a Republican Party rally, we may assume he has a positive attitude toward the Republican Party. We might assume, then, that the individual himself may make similar inferences about his attributes, and as the voluminous literature on conformity and demand characteristics of situations makes clear, people do indeed sometimes describe themselves in the ways they believe they are expected to be. It would seem, then, that in inferring his attributes, an individual has at least two potential sources of information: (1) those things he does, or rather, his perception of what he does, *self-produced cues*, and (2) those things, usually socially mediated, which the situation imply he is, the *situationally-produced cues*. A man may decide he is happy because he is smiling or because he is at a party.

The question arises whether self-produced cues are dominant over situational cues or vice versa. Schachter and his associates have found that overweight and normally weighted people use different kinds of cues in attributing "hunger" to themselves (Schachter, 1967). Normally weighted people eat in response to self-produced cues such as gastric motility, while overweight people use situational cues to govern eating.

The study reported here[1] represents an attempt to test the possibility that differences in the use of self vs. situationally produced cues may occur in other self-attribution situations. The study grew out of the observation that in the study described earlier (Laird, in press) some *S*s seemed to respond strongly to the manipulation of facial expression while others responded little or not at all. The response of *S*s could have been a chance occurrence, but it could also have represented a consistent difference between individuals.

If the tendency to respond to the self-produced cues of the facial expression manipulation is an enduring characteristic, then one might expect the same individuals to respond or not respond to the expression manipulations each time they are exposed to them. If, on the other hand, response is due to chance, individuals will not be expected to respond similarly on different occasions. The basic procedure of the present study, then, was to manipulate facial expression on two different occasions, separated by about two days. We postulate that (a) *S*s whose emotional experience is affected by their expressive behavior on one day will be similarly affected on the second; (b) there will exist consistent differences in everyday experiences of emotion between *S*s who do and do not respond consistently to the manipulation of expressive behavior. To test this latter point, a series of questions relating to emotional experience were asked of *S*s.

METHOD

Subjects

Subjects were 32 undergraduate student volunteers, 17 men and 15 women. Six were subsequently excluded because they revealed awareness of the experimental hypothesis. The final group consisted of 13 men and 13 women.

Procedure

The procedure for manipulating facial expression followed closely that used by Laird (in press). In brief, the procedure involves a deception intended to convey the impression that the experiment is concerned with physiological activity during visual perception. The expression manipulations were presented as part of the physiological measurement procedures, and the emotion measures as controls for experimental error; thus, neither was presented as a central part of the ostensible purpose of the experiment.

*S*s were told that the experiment was concerned with "the activity of the facial muscles during perception" and were told that the activity of their facial muscles was to be recorded through six silver cup electrodes which were attached to their faces. The ostensible task of the *S*s was simply to sit and look at the stimuli. It was explained, however, that emotional fluctuations might introduce a possible source of error through their effect on the muscle potential recordings. Consequently, *S*s were asked to report their feelings during each trial, being particularly alert, since "We normally have moment-to-moment, almost random fluctuations in mood that we ordinarily pay no attention to." While the electrodes were being attached, it was explained that the physiological measurements were to be of two kinds, on resting muscles and on muscles under contraction. Consequently, *S*s would be asked to contract and relax various muscles on different trials.

After the electrodes were attached to *S*'s face, at each corner of the jaw, on either side of the midline between the eyebrows, and approximately one inch later to and slightly above each corner of the mouth, the first trial was begun.

The first step in each trial was the arrangement of the *S*'s face into either a "smile" or a "frown." To obtain the expressions, the experimenter stood in front of the *S*, and asked him to contract various muscles. For the "frown" position, *S*s were asked to contract the muscles under the electrodes between their eyebrows, by "drawing the brows together and down," and to contract the muscles at the corners of their jaws by "clenching (their) teeth." For the "smile" position, *S*s were asked to contract the muscles under the electrodes near the corners of their mouths by "drawing the corners of (their) mouth back and up."

When the experimenter was satisfied with the expression, one of four cartoons was projected on a screen in front of the subjects. The cartoons had been used as visual stimuli in a previous experiment and had been equated for humor. A different set of four cartoons were employed in each replication. The pairing of cartoons with expression conditions in each replication was counterbalanced.

After subjects had viewed the cartoons for 15 seconds, the projector was shut off, the experimenter gave *S* a brief MACL form (Nowlis, 1968) and reminded him, "Be sure to use this to describe how you felt during the time you were looking at the stimulus."

Each *S* had one trial in the frown condition and one in the smile condition. Half of the *S*s received a frown trial first, and half received a smile trial first.

The procedure was repeated in a second session for all *S*s. For most *S*s, there was a period of two days between sessions. Two *S*s were unable to appear two days after the first session, and their second session occurred three days after the initial session.

Following both sessions, *S*s filled out a post-experimental questionnaire. If they perceived a causal relationship between their experimentally manipulated expressions and their feelings, this knowledge might have influenced their response on the dependent measures. For this reason, *S*s revealing this awareness at either session were excluded from the final analysis. The questionnaire employed to assess awareness of the purposes and procedures of the experiment consisted of six questions asking *S*s to describe the purpose of the experiment, why they felt their mood changed, and if the muscle contractions had affected them in any way.

Responses to these questions were evaluated independently by two judges who agreed that six *S*s were aware of a relationship between the experimental manipulations and their feelings. These six were excluded from subsequent analyses.

The Mood Adjective Check List employed was a brief form derived from the Nowlis-Green Mood Adjective Check List (Nowlis, 1968). It consisted of three adjectives drawn from the Elation factor (Carefree, Elated, Pleased) and three from the Aggression factor (Angry, Annoyed, Defiant).

Within each trial, the principal variable consisted of a summary score derived from the six mood adjectives. Scores on the Elation adjectives were assigned positive values, scores on the Aggression adjectives were assigned negative values, and these scores were then added to yield an emotional response score in which a positive score indicated *S* was feeling relatively happy while a negative score indicated he was feeling relatively angry. The emotional response score was obtained for each trial, and comparisons of these scores for the "frown" and "smile" trials provided an estimate of the degree to which *S*s' MACL scores differed as a function of the manipulations within each replication.

To obtain a single score representing the extent of the effect of the manipulation of expression for each replication as a whole, the emotional response score for the "frown" trial was subtracted from the same score for the "smile" trial, to yield a single score for each *S* for each replication. Thus an *S* who exhibited a strong expression effect might have had a score of +4 on the "smile" trial and a -4 on the "frown" trial, producing an overall expression effect score of +4 - (-4) = +8. This score summarizes the expression effect for each replication. Positive scores mean that *S* was happier on "smile" trials and/or angrier on "frown" trials. Negative scores indicate that *S* tended to be happier on "frown" trials than on "smile" trials or angrier on "smile" trials.

At the conclusion of the second replication, *S*s responded to a series of questions concerning their emotional experience. Four questions made up an emotional experience questionnaire. These four questions were derived on the assumption that people who utilized self-produced cues more extensively in attributing emotions to themselves would respond differently in certain situations from people who utilized situational cues. *S*s responded to each question on an eleven-point scale. The questions, and their specific rationales were as follows

1. "How frequently do other people misjudge how you feel? That is, how often do other people seem to think you feel one way when you actually feel very differently?" The rationale here is that the expressive behavior of others is probably more difficult to judge than situational definitions of "appropriateness," which must necessarily be consensual. Hence, people whose emotional experience is a product of the self-produced cues of expressive behavior will more commonly be misunderstood.

2. "How often do you find that you feel differently from those around you? For example, when you are in a group of people who seem happy, do you often feel sad or angry or some other emotion than happiness?" The rationale of this question is that subjects who use situational cues will rarely feel themselves to be at variance with a particular situation.

3. "How often do you have feelings for which you can see no clear object or reason? That is, how often do you experience an emotion and have no clear idea why you feel that way?" Reasons and explanations in our culture are almost always defined in terms of external objects and situational events. Hence, people who use situational cues will presumably always be able to explain their emotional experiences in terms of the situational "reasons" for it. On the other hand, people who use self-produced cues may well occasionally be expressing, and hence feeling, an emotion not clearly justified by the situation.

4. "Frequently one moves from a situation in which one is feeling one way to a situation in which it is appropriate to feel some other way, as for instance when you have an argument with someone and then immediately must be with someone else. How rapidly and easily do you change from the first kind of feeling to the second?" Here the assumption is that the processes which produce expressive behavior are essentially automatic and seem to take a moderate amount of time to decline. This "lag"

in response will lead to difficulty in changing situations. The person who responds to situational cues, on the other hand, will change readily.

Scores on these four questions were summed to produce a score which may be considered to represent the relative dominance of situational or self-produced cues. Higher scores indicate greater use of situational cues. The individual items were also analyzed separately.

A final, separately analyzed question was aimed at a more direct report of the difference in cue utilization. The use of self-produced cues seems to be a much more immediate and unself-conscious process of attribution, so much so that people often deny that it occurs even in the face of evidence. The use of situational cues, on the other hand, seems to imply a rather different experience of the process of emotional attribution. It seemed likely, then, that people predominantly using one kind of cue or another would report a different kind of experience of their emotions. To test this, *S*s were asked whether their everyday experience of an emotion was more nearly "like a sensation: the emotional feelings are immediately and strongly experienced, like the color red in a red object," or more nearly "like a judgment: the emotional feelings are experienced as appropriate to the circumstances, in the way that one knows that a particular action in those circumstances would be right or wrong."

RESULTS

Although this study is concerned with the consistency of expression effects across replications, the extent of expression effect within each replication may also be examined. Since both replications were reasonably approximate replications of studies reported earlier (Laird, in press), similar results may be anticipated. That is, it may be predicted that, considering the whole sample, in each replication *S*s will report feeling more happy and less angry on "smile" trials and the converse for"frown" trials. In the first replication this prediction was not confirmed. The mean emotion score on the "smile" trials was 2.23, and, on the "frown" trials, 2.38, an insignificant difference. In replication II the difference was in the direction predicted, and significantly replicated the earlier studies. The mean emotion score on the "smile" trials was 3.19, and, on the "frown" trials, 1.04 ($t = 1.78$, $p < .05$, one-tailed).[2] There were no significant differences between male and female *S*s.

While these results only partially replicated the earlier studies, they did not present any difficulty with respect to the purpose of this study. The hypothesis to be tested in this study was, in effect, that some individuals will respond, as in the earlier studies, and some will not. In light of this hypothesis, earlier positive results may be interpreted as in part a consequence of the providential fact that there were a sufficiently large number of subjects of the first kind in the samples employed. The weaker results of the present study may be interpreted as due to a sample containing a smaller proportion than earlier samples of the hypothesized "kind" of person who responds to such manipulations. On the assumption that this sample nonetheless contained at least some of this "kind" of individual, who responds to self-produced cues, it remains feasible to examine the consistency of responses across both replications.

The expression effect score for each replication consisted of two theoretically distinct components. The sign of the score, positive, negative, or zero, represented whether, in general, *S*s were happier when "smiling," sadder when "frowning," and so forth. Thus, the sign of the score represents whether *S*s responded consistently with the hypotheses concerning the experimental manipulations. The absolute magnitude of the score, on the other hand, represented the intensity of the emotional experience. According to the theory guiding this research, intensity is a function of degree of physiological arousal (Schachter, 1964; Laird, in press), which was uncontrolled in the present situation. Thus, to treat the expression effect scores as continuous would be to include as "error" the variance due to these uncontrolled differences between replications in degree of arousal. As a consequence, the expression effect scores were collapsed to two categories, positive expression effect, including all positive scores, and no expression effect, including both zero and negative scores.

Whether *S*s had positive or non-positive expression

effect scores was highly consistent across the two replications. The relevant data are presented in Table 4.1. In the first replication, 11 *S*s had positive expression effect scores, while 15 had zero or negative scores. In the second replication 16 *S*s had positive expression effect scores, including 10 of the 11 who had positive scores in the first replication. The association between the two replications, examined using Fischer Exact Test (Siegel, 1956), reached accepted levels of confidence ($p < .05$, two-tailed).

TABLE 4.1. Subjects with Positive and Non-positive Expression Effect Scores for Replications I and II.

		Replication II Scores	
		Zero or Negative	*Positive*
Replication I Scores	*Zero or Negative*	9	6
	Positive	1	10

Note: $p < .05$, 2-tailed, by Fisher Exact Test.

The ten *S*s who received positive expression effect scores on both replications were designated the expression effect group and were compared with the other *S*s, the inconsistent or anti-expression effect group, with respect to scores on the emotional experience measures. As will be recalled, a high score indicates relatively great use of situational cues.

The mean total emotional experience score for the expression effect group was 20.00, and the mean for the inconsistent or anti-effect group was 23.69. This difference was statistically significant ($t = 2.16$, $p < .05$, two-tailed). These data are summarized in Table 4.2, along with scores on the individual items.

The two groups also differed significantly in the description of their experience of an emotion. The relevant data are summarized in Table 4.3. Positive expression-effect *S*s tended to describe their experience of emotion as more like a sensation, and the no-expression-

TABLE 4.2. Responses to Emotional Experience Questions of Positive and Non-positive Expression Effect Groups.

Question	*Positive Group Mean*	*Non-positive Group Mean*	*t*
1.	6.20	6.31	<1.0
2.	5.60	6.25	<1.0
3.	3.40	5.19	1.79*
4.	4.70	5.94	1.31
Total of Responses to Emotional Experience Questions	20.00	23.69	2.16**

*$p < .10$, 2-tailed
**$p < .05$, 2-tailed

effect group tended to describe their experience as more like a judgment ($p < .05$, two-tailed, by Fisher Exact Test).

TABLE 4.3. Description of Emotional Experience by Positive and Non-positive Expression Effect Groups.

	Description	
Groups	*"Like a sensation"*	*"Like a judgment"*
Positive Expression Effect	9	1
Non-positive Expression Effect	7	9

Note: $p < .05$, 2-tailed, by Fisher Exact Test.

DISCUSSION

While not anticipated, the failure of the first replication to replicate earlier results is consistent with the individual differences hypothesis of the present study. Implicit in the individual differences hypothesis is the assumption that, through chance or some unnoticed selection variable, samples of *S*s may sometimes contain a relatively small proportion of individuals who customarily employ self-produced cues in self-attribution. In these instances, significant self-attribution effects over the whole group will not be observed. That the second replication did replicate earlier results is equally consistent with the individual difference hypothesis and with earlier work (Laird, in press). However, the differences between the two replications, involving the same individual *S*s, is less clearly consistent with the hypothesis suggested here, particularly since other analyses and data support the view that there are consistent individual differences in the use of expression cues.

The results may be most reasonably interpreted by expanding the conception of what differences in cue use involve. The argument thus far has simply been that, with respect to cues used in self-attribution, there are two kinds of people, those who attribute personal qualities to themselves on the basis of their own behavior, and those who attribute personal qualities on the basis of other, presumably situational, cues. This conception is undoubtedly simple-minded. It is more reasonable to suppose that every individual, depending on the circumstances, may use either self-produced or situational cues. Differences between people consist only of the relative importance of the different cue classes. Undoubtedly, in some extreme situations, when no situational cues are available, everyone will respond in terms of self-produced cues, and, at the other extreme, if self-produced cues for some reason are unavailable, everyone will employ situational cues. Between these extremes, when both kinds of cues are available, the hypothesized individual differences in cue use might be expected to occur.

Further, in any new situation we might imagine that people spend some effort in trying to find out what is expected. In the experimental situation used in the present study, despite the cartoons, the situational cues for emotion were minimal, and initially indicated that no particular emotion, except perhaps mild humor, was expected. Thus, particularly during the first replication, to the extent that *S*s were attending to the situation, they would have attended less to their "self-produced" cues, of the expression manipulation, and hence would show less of an expression effect. As they became more accustomed to the situation, in the second replication, they may have attended less to the situation and more to the expression manipulations, and hence have showed an expression effect. This explanation is, of course, speculative, but seems consistent with the results and the hypotheses.

If this explanation is accurate, then a further prediction concerning the individual differences analysis is implied. The notion of relative weighting of self-produced versus situational cues implies that those *S*s who did respond to the expression manipulations in the first replication would be those who customarily gave greatest weight to self-produced cues. Thus, it might be expected that, in the second replication, where the circumstances were more favorable to attention to self-produced cues, all or almost all of these *S*s would respond again, while some *S*s who did not respond in the first replication would now respond. That is, or course, precisely the pattern of results observed. Ten of the 11 *S*s who responded to the first replication responded to the second, as did 6 *S*s who did not respond the first time.

With respect to the central focus of this study, then, the results supported the hypothesis that individuals differ in their response to manipulation of their expressive behavior. To a statistically significant extent, *S*s who responded to the expression manipulations on one occasion, responded on a second occasion, while those who failed to respond on one occasion were unlikely to respond on a second. It is clear that whether an *S* responded or not to this particular set of experimental manipulations was a consistent difference between individuals.

It might have been, however, that this difference represented some kind of error which happened to be consistent between the two replications. For instance, in as much as it is difficult to pose people's faces "realistically" in the procedure used, perhaps the differences observed were simply between the people easily posed and those more difficult to pose. Such an interpretation of the results can never be completely rejected, but it seems unlikely in light of the results with respect to the emotion experience questions. These questions were generated from the differential cue use hypothesis. *S*s' responses to these questions and to the expression manipulations were significantly related in a theoretically consistent manner. It is difficult to imagine how the differences between the expression effect group and the no-effect group could be explained except by this kind of hypothesis.

The most plausible interpretation of the entire pattern of results, then, seems to be that people do indeed vary with respect to their response to this particular variety of self-produced cues, facial expressions. In other words, for some people, the emotions they feel are a function of the expressive behavior in which they are engaging, while for others, expressive behavior has little or no effect upon emotional experience. This latter group, it has been argued, may experience emotions as a function of what they understand to be the situational expectations or norms for emotional experience. This interpretation is to some degree supported by the fact that subjects who did not respond to the expression manipulations tended to describe their emotional experience as "like a judgment;...the emotional feelings are experienced as *appropriate to the circumstances*, in the way that one knows that a particular action in those circumstances would be right or wrong." Subjects who endorsed this alternative seem to be describing just the kind of mediation of emotional experience that has been postulated. However, the relationships between responses to this item and to the expression manipulations may have been produced by the differential attractiveness of the other alternative to the two expression effect groups. That is,the no-effect group may have endorsed the "judgment" alternative as inaccurate but closer to their experience than the only other alternative given them. In sum, then, these results support the hypothesis that individuals vary in the degree to which self-produced cues of this kind mediate their experience, but the related hypothesis, that the other kind of cue used is situational, remains a hypothesis, to be entertained because it seems the most reasonable possibility.

One obvious implication of these results is that it would be fruitful to study other self-attribution phenomena and classes of self-produced cues to see if similar differences in cue usage prevail. It seems probable that just as only some people respond to manipulations of expressive behavior, so also only some people respond to "forced" attitude or belief statements, or to variations in level of physiological arousal.

NOTES

1. This research was in part supported by NSF/URP grant #GY 4179.
2. The use of a one-tailed test is justified here since this analysis represents a replication and is the test of a specific, directional hypothesis.

REFERENCES

Bem, D.J. 1967. Self perception: An alternative interpretation of cognitive dissonance phenomena. *Psychological Review* 74:183-200.

Festinger, L. 1957. *A Theory of Cognitive Dissonance*. Evanston, Ill.: Row, Peterson.

Festinger, L., and Carlsmith, J.M. 1959. Cognitive consequences of forced compliance. *Journal of Abnormal and Social Psychology* 58:203-210.

Laird, J.D. 1967. The effect of facial expression on emotional experience. Paper presented at Eastern Psychological Association meetings.

----. In press. Self-attribution of emotion: The effects of expressive behavior on the quality of emotional experience. *Journal of Personality and Social Psychology*.

Nowlis, V. 1968. Research with the mood adjective check list. *In* Tomkins, S., and Izard, C. (eds.), *Affect: Measurement of Awareness and Performance*. New York: Springer.

Schachter, S. 1964. The interaction of cognitive and physiological determinants of emotional state. *In* L. Berkowitz (ed.), *Advances in Experimental Social Psychology,* Vol. 1. New York: Academic Press.

----. 1967. Cognitive effects on bodily functioning:

Studies of obesity and eating. *In* D.C. Glass (ed.), *Neurophysiology and Emotion.* New York: Rockefeller University Press.

Schachter, S., and Singer, J. 1962. Cognitive, social and physiological determinants of emotional state. *Psychological Review* 69:379-399.

Siegel, S. 1956. *Nonparametric Statistics for the Behavioral Sciences.* New York: McGraw-Hill.

5

Karl P. Koenig and
Kermit Henriksen

Cognitive Manipulation of GSR Extinction: Analogues for Conditioning Therapies

Cognitive determinants of GSR activity during extinction trials were examined following conditioning. Conditioned GSRs extinguished rapidly when subjects were informed the UCS would not again be administered, compared to subjects not given this information. Of greater interest was the finding that (false) high feedback concerning subjects' responsivity to the CS+ during extinction served to maintain GSR activity at a higher level than subjects receiving (false) low feedback. The relationship was observed within both information conditions. Implications are drawn for both aversive conditioning therapy and systematic desensitization.

The methods of conditioning therapies rest upon certain assumptions concerning the acquisition and extinction of conditioned emotional responses and principally those responses associated with the construct of anxiety. Aversion therapy consists of the acquisition of noxious emotional responses which in turn provide motivation to sustain the avoidance of some set of undesirable instrumental behaviors. Its success, therefore, depends heavily upon resistance of the conditioned emotional response to extinction. Systematic desensitization, on the other hand, is effective to the extent that maladaptive conditioned emotional behavior can be rapidly extinguished.

Evidence is available which indicates that extinction of conditioned emotional behavior is precipitated when subjects are informed that the UCS will no longer occur. This relationship has been demonstrated in heart-rate conditioning (Chatterjee and Erikson, 1962; Notterman, Schoenfeld,aand Bersh, 1952) and in GSR conditioning (Bridger and Mandel, 1965; Cook and Harris, 1937; Koenig and del Castillo, 1969; Mowrer, 1938; Silverman, 1960; Wickens, Allen, and Hill, 1963). Given this frequently replicated phenomenon in human subjects, and the obvious similarity to aversion therapy during which clients are generally aware when an aversive event is probable and when it is not, it is not surprising that Feldman (1966) was less than sanguine about the successes of aversion therapy. Rapid extinction of conditioned emotional behavior will be the rule unless procedures are followed which interfere with the subjects' perceptions of the likelihood of UCS occurrence.

A recent investigation of manipulated GSR feedback in an aversion therapy analogue found that extinction can be retarded even when subjects are fully informed that UCS probability is equal to zero (Koenig and del Castillo, 1969). Resistance to extinction was achieved by leading subjects to believe (incorrectly) that activity of a visible meter was an accurate reflection of their GSRs to conditioned stimuli during non-shocked trials.

The present study[1] attempted to replicate the above finding and to test more broadly the effects of false feedback. Specifically, it was predicted that feedback indicating high emotionality would result in slower extinction rates than feedback indicative of low emotionality. It was further predicted that the difference between the two feedback conditions would appear as a clear effect *within* the informed and non-informed conditions when analyzed separately.

The design of the study included two levels of information (informed and non-informed) and two levels of feedback (low and high). In addition, two smaller and supplementary control groups were run. One control consisted of non-informed subjects who received low feedback meter readings but for whom the readings were meaningless. The second control was comprised of informed subjects who received high feedback meter readings and for whom the readings were also meaningless. The major purpose of the controls was to discover whether meter readings per se would produce acceleration or retardation of extinction. It was predicted that they would not.

METHOD

Subjects

The sample consisted of 70 undergraduate students enrolled in an introductory course in psychology. To each of four experimental conditions, 15 subjects were assigned. To both of two control conditions, five subjects were assigned. All subjects were assigned randomly.

Apparatus

A Lafayette dermohmeter (7601A) was used in conjunction with a Harvard Electronic Recording Module (350) to produce a continuous ink recording of resistance change. A second pen recorded time and stimulus events. The equipment, including timers, relays, and shock stimulator, was located in a control room connected by a two-way mirror to the subject room.

Nickel-plated finger electrodes were taped to sub ject's first and third right-hand fingers and connected to the dermohmeter. His right arm was secured by an elastic bandage to the arm of a recliner chair to reduce GSR artifacts. Shock was delivered to the left hand in .5-second impulses in a range of .0-5.5mA. through a 100-KΩ resistor in series with subject.

The subject sat in a small but comfortable room. A headset and intercom permitted two-way communication with experimenter. The chair faced a panel of three jewel lights, 4.5 feet away at eye level, and visible through the two-way mirror when illuminated. Lights were timed for 2-second durations. The reinforced light (positive conditioned stimulus, CS+) was orange, while the nonreinforced stimuli (negative conditioned stimuli, CSs-) consisted of two white lights equal in size and brightness to the CS+. The CS+ was easily discriminable from the CSs-. All stimuli and intervals were controlled by automated apparatus.

Also visible, when illuminated by experimenter during extinction trials, was a 4 X 3 inch black-on-white meter set 4 inches below the lights. The meter needle movements were under the control of the experimenter and are described in the next section.

Procedures

1. *Adaptation*. Five CSs+ (without UCS) and 10 CSs- were presented in a fixed random order with a fixed random order of inter-trial intervals (15, 20, or 25 seconds).

2. *UCS determination*. An unpleasant, but tolerable, level of shock was found for each subject. The obtained range of tolerances was .5 to 5.5 mA.

3. *Acquisition*. Ten CSs+ and 20 CSs- were presented in a new fixed-random order with variable inter-trial intervals. Each CS+ was followed immediately by a shock of .5 second duration 100% of the time. After all 30 stimuli were presented, an eleventh CS+ without shock was presented to determine conditioning (test trial).

4. *Extinction*. Twelve CSs+ and 24 CSs- were presented in a new order with a new set of inter-trial intervals. No shock was delivered at any time during extinction trials for any subject.

No differential conditions were introduced until the extinction phase.

Information conditions. Following the test trial, but prior to extinction trials, one-half of the subjects received instructions designed to assure them that the remaining stimulus presentations would not involve shock. Abstracted, instructions for the informed subjects were as follows: "I am coming in now to remove the shock electrodes. From this point on, none of the lights will be followed by shock." The experimenter then joined the subject and removed the shock electrodes.

The remaining shbjects received no indication that shock would be terminated. To control for experimenter's interruption, however, these subjects (non-informed) were told that an adjustment was to be made in the amplifying system. The experimenter then entered the room and appeared to make such an adjustment.

Feedback conditions. Two groups of 15 subjects received high feedback and two groups of 15 subjects received low feedback. Meter activity began immediately upon termination of each CS+ during the first six extinction trials and ended seven seconds after onset of the activity. In the high-feedback conditions, subjects were exposed, therefore, to a series of six opportunities to view meter activity, the peak meter values being 45, 57, 45, 50, 53, and 43. Subjects in the low-feedback conditions saw a series of meter readings whose peak values were 23, 15, 17, 5, 10, and 12. In order to make the meter activity "realistic," hesitations in the needle rise and fall were also programmed into the schedule.

Subjects in the feedback conditions were given the following instructions at the onset of extinction trials. "I will continue to present the lights to you now. Please pay close attention to the lights. During this part of the experiment, you will sometimes be able to see your own GSR response, just as our instruments are actually recording it here in the control room. Can you see the meter? Each time the orange light goes *off*, it will then turn *on* the needle of the meter. If your body produces a GSR it will show up on the meter within a few seconds. The needle typically rises slowly and peaks between the values of 25 to 35 with 30 being the average value for most college students of your sex. When the needle returns, the mechanism is automatically switched off, until the next orange light occurs." (This message was repeated again in order to ensure that the subject understood what the "average" student's response was.)

After six CS+ presentations, the subject was told that, "I am going to switch off the needle mechanism now, but the meter light will stay on for the rest of the experiment."

High and low values control groups. A group of five subjects experienced a condition parallel to that of non-informed subjects who received low feedback except that these subjects were not instructed about the meaning of the meter activity. They were merely asked to attend carefully to the meter in order to answer some questions.

about it later. The meter was manipulated exactly as in the regular low-feedback conditions.

A second group of five subjects served as a control for the high-feedback informed subjects, but without instructions about how to interpret the significance of the meter activity. The meter values, however, corresponded to those in the high-feedback conditions.

RESULTS

The GSR unit changes associated with each CS+ during extinction trials were converted from changes in resistance to log changes in conductance consistent with suggestions by Haggard (1949) and Lacey and Siegel (1949). The raw response measure consisted of the maximum resistance change (ohms) within an 8-second period after CS+ termination. Positive log CCs reflect decrements in skin resistance. A constant of 1 was added to each change value before the logarithmic transformation was made.

A trend analysis of variance was performed upon data from the four groups of principal experimental interest. The analysis is summarized in Table 5.1 and the extinction responses are shown in Figures 5.1 and 5.2 together with control groups data. A one-way analysis of variance was calculated for test-trial data in order to verify the assumption that no real differences existed among the groups prior to the introduction of experimental variables. No significant differences were found.

A convincing replication of differential extinction rates due to information about the onset of non-shocked trials was obtained ($F = 47.18$). The establishment of this phenomenon was necessary for a clear interpretation of differential effects attributable to high and low feedback within the two information conditions.

Consistent with the prediction made earlier, the main effect for feedback was significant ($F = 7.94$), indicating that low feedback tended generally to produce a lower overall rate of response during extinction and that high feedback produced a higher rate. The means for extinction trials within the informed condition were 1.26 (high feedback) and .76 (low feedback). The means differed significantly ($t = 2.15$, $df = 28$, $p < .025$, 1-tailed test). Within the non-informed condition, the overall means were 2.59 (high feedback) and 2.01 (low feedback) which was significant at the .05 level (t = 1.95, df = 28, 1-tailed test). These results support the generality of the feedback effect.

TABLE 5.1. Analysis of Variance of Log. Change in Conductance as a Function of Information and Meter Feedback.

	d.f.	*M.S.*	*F*
Feedback (F)		50.93	7.94*
Information (I)		302.47	47.18*
F X I	1	.26	--
Error a.	56	6.41	
Trials (T)	11	10.48	10.92*
T X F	11	1.60	--
T X I	11	.92	--
T X I X F	11	1.15	--
Error b.	616	.96	

*$p < .01$.

Figures 5.1 and 5.2 show, in addition to the major effects described above, the plotted functions of two control groups. In Figure 5.1 it may be seen that control subjects receiving high meter values, without knowledge of the meaning of the values, rapidly approached a zero level of responding, a level well below even those subjects receiving meaningful low feedback. Consequently, high meter values per se did not retard extinction of the conditioned emotional response. The performance of control subjects shown in Figure 5.2, however, was less clear-cut. These subjects tended to occupy an intermediate position between the experimental groups until the offset of meter feedback. One might argue that the control condition should have produced the maximum emotional response, relative to all other non-informed groups, but it did so only for the last six CS presentations. Subjects in this condition were required to cope with more ambituity than those in other conditions because they were increasingly unsure whether additional shock would be forthcoming and they were given no information about themselves to process. It should be noted, however, that considerable separation was obtained between the control group and the group with which a comparison was intended, the non-informed low-feedback group.

In addition to the establishment of a reliable main effect associated with high and low feedback, a trials X feedback interaction was also expected. An interaction would indicate that feedback affected extinction rates differentially over trials. The interaction failed to reach statistical significance when all trials or the first six trials were analyzed. An analysis of the last six trials, however, yielded a significant trials X feedback interaction ($F = 2.57$, $df = 5, 280$, $p < .05$).

DISCUSSION

Convincing information that an unpleasant shock associated with the offset of a stimulus light would not occur again produced rapid decay of a conditioned GSR relative to a second condition which did not present subjects with such information. The importance of this finding for those who would engage in complex manipulations of human anxiety for therapeutic ends has already been mentioned. The study has also shown that the cognitive variable of information vs. no information can nonetheless be interfered with to a significant extent. Indeed, the data suggest that the human subject is quite receptive to information he receives about his emotional status, and responds in conformity to the general configuration of the feedback. In short, a subject who receives the impression that his emotional response level is above "average" tends to respond at a higher emotional level than a subject who is led to believe that his emotional response level is below "average." The control group data add further to this interpretation to the extent that high or low meter activity, without the subject's knowledge of the meaning of the activity, produced extinction curves different from those of subjects who had this knowledge.

Three interpretations of these findings should be explored. The first assumes that a person can serve as his own model for imitative responses. Since it has been demonstrated that emotional responses can be both acquired

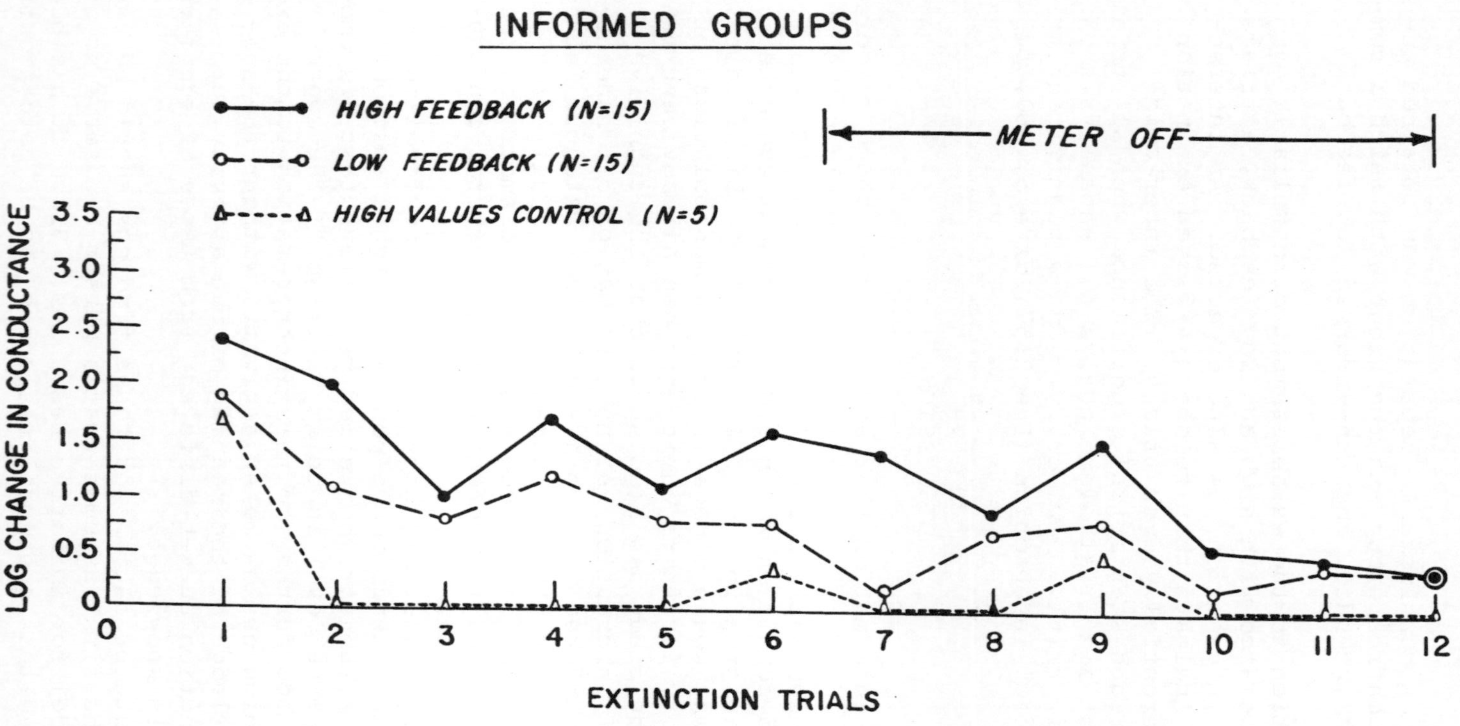

FIGURE 5.1. Extinction curves.

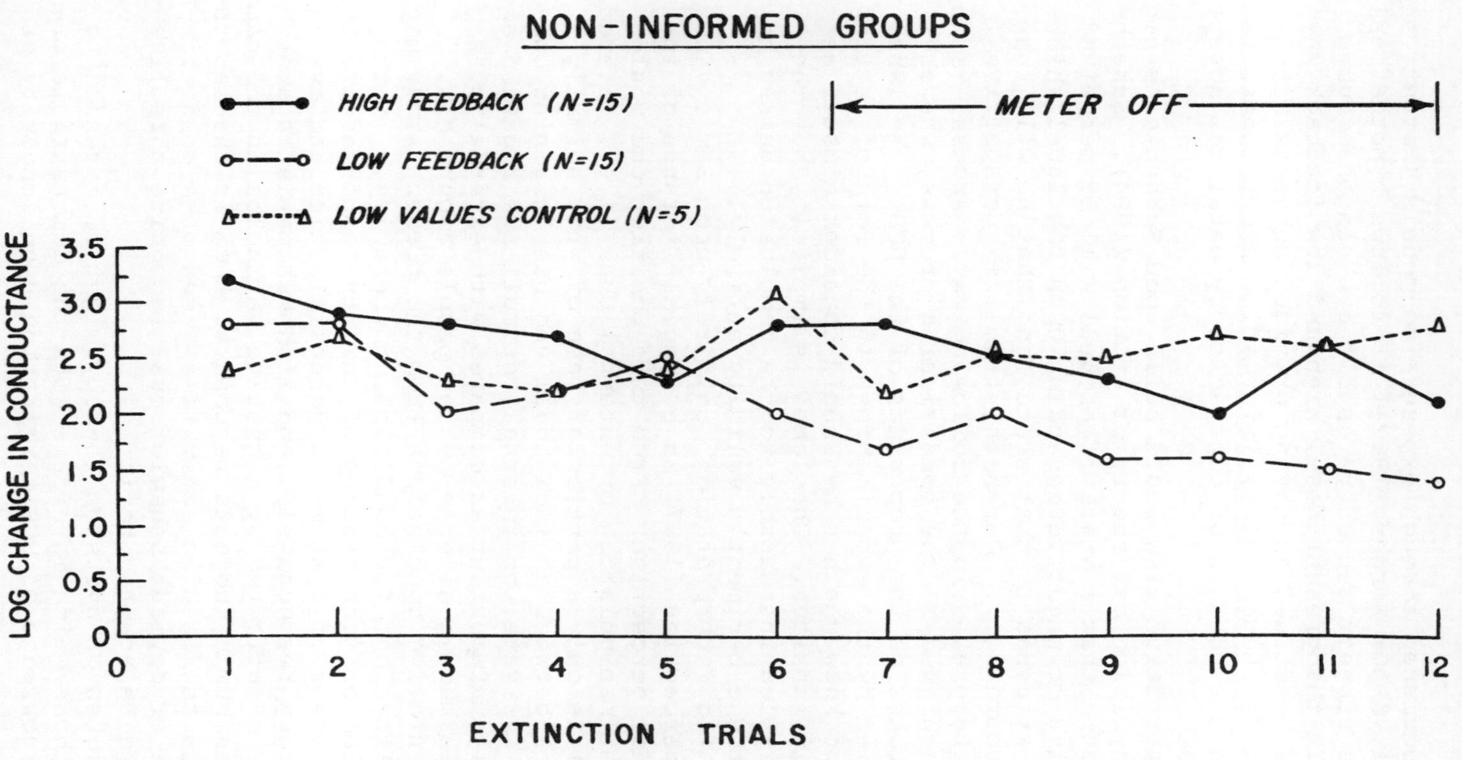

FIGURE 5.2. Extinction curves.

and extinguished through exposure to models (Barnett and Benedetti, 1960; Berger, 1962), it follows hypothetically that a subject can serve as his own response cuing model. In the present case, high and low feedback may simply be construed as having provided subjects with processed (although false) information about themselves which, in the absence of contradictory data, was accepted as true.

An alternative view would build upon Schachter's cognitive-physiological theory of emotion (1964). Schachter suggests that a state of arousal will be perceived as positive or negative depending upon the label which a person attaches to that state, and that he will then behave accordingly. Our data, from this perspective, may be interpreted in the following way. Arousal is initially achieved by the conditioning process, whereby the CS+ takes on the properties of the UCS. The label is supplied by the experimenters in the form of letting the person know whether he should consider himself as high or low anxious. The label is implicit, but the subject is led inescapably to the conclusion unless he rejects the e periment's validity entirely.

A related interpretation would rely upon Bem's view of self-perception (1967) as a special instance of interpersonal perception. From this position one would argue that manipulation of external cues (i.e., metered feedback) is only a particular case of what normally transpires between an individual and his "training community." Private, or internal, stimuli are regarded as relatively unimportant as compared with external cues and labels made available by the people around him.

The tentative conclusions from the present study may have implications for conditioning therapies. If the elimination or conditioning of anxiety responses are the core processes of systematic desensitization and aversion therapy respectively, and if human patients are likely to be affected by cognitive variables in the same fashion as human subjects respond to them in the laboratory, then therepeutic activities based on a conditioning model of deviant behavior must recognize this likelihood and be adapted to it.

Techniques of aversion therapy might be extended to include those which interfere with the demonstrable effect of knowledge of UCS termination upon longevity of the conditioned response. This chapter and an earlier report (Koenig and del Castillo, 1969) indicate that false high feedback concerning emotional responsivity will produce such interference. The application of the feedback principle within aversion therapy might involve, in addition to CS-UCS pairing, many non-shocked trials during which the subject (e.g., a homosexual or an alcoholic) receives "scientific" verification of his continued strong emotional response to the CS. We would reason on the basis of findings reported here that such a procedure would tend to maintain aversion to the CS for a longer period of time than would conventional treatment.

Systematic desensitization is applied when individuals remain highly anxious in the presence of stimuli which are objectively non-threatening. It may be useful to consider such anxiety as roughly analogous to that established in the present study by failing to inform subjects that extinction trials have commenced (i.e., that UCS probability = 0). Clients who receive systematic desensitization treatments do so because they have persisted in behaving as though UCS probability is greater, often much greater, than zero. The present study suggests that subjects given evidence that they are acting non-anxiously do, in fact, act less anxiously than subjects told the opposite or nothing. While the effect was not powerful enough to reduce the conditioned response to zero (in twelve trials), the results suggest that an additional dimension to be investigated in desensitization might well be therapist-manipulated emotional feedback. Similar reasoning was employed in a study by Valins and Ray (1967). By using false heart-rate feedback (auditory), they were able to change approach behavior to a feared stimulus.

NOTES

1. This research was supported by Research Grant MH-12854-02. Acknowledgement is owed to Harry Linneman and Lawrence Dickerson for their assistance in the experiment.

Requests for reprints should be sent to Karl P. Koenig, Department of Psychology, University of New Mexico, Albuquerque, New Mexico, 87106.

REFERENCES

Barnett, P.E., and Benedetti, D.T. 1960. A study in "vicarious conditioning." Paper presented at the meeting of the Rocky Mountain Psychological Association, Glenwood Springs, Colorado.

Bem, Daryl J. 1967. Self perception: An alternative interpretation of cognitive dissonance phenomena. *Psychological Review* 74:183-200.

Berger, S.M. 1962. Conditioning through vicarious instigation. *Psychological Review* 69:450-466.

Bridger, W.H., and Mandel, I.J. 1965. Abolition of the PRE by instructions in GSR conditioning. *Journal of Experimental Psychology* 69:476-482.

Chatterjee, B.B., and Ericksen, C.W. 1962. Cognitive factors in heart-rate conditioning. *Journal of Experimental Psychology* 64:272-279.

Cook, S.W., and Harris, R.E. 1937. The verbal conditioning of the galvanic skin reflex. *Journal of Experimental Psychology* 21:202-210.

Feldman, M.P. 1966. Aversion therapy for sexual deviations: A critical review. *Psychological Bulletin* 65: 65-79.

Haggard, E.A. 1949. On the application of analysis of variance to GSR data: I. The selection of an appropriate measure. *Journal of Experimental Psychology* 39:378-392.

Koenig, K.P., and del Castillo, D. 1969. False feedback and longevity of the conditioned GSR during extinction: Some implications for aversion therapy. *Journal of Abnormal Psychology* 74:505-510.

Lacey, O.L., and Siegel, P.S. 1949. An analysis of the unit of measurement of the galvanic skin response. *Journal of Experimental Psychology* 39:122-127.

Mowrer, O.H. 1938. Preparatory set (expectancy)--a determinant in motivation and learning. *Psychological Review* 45:62-91.

Notterman, J.M., Schoenfeld, W.W., and Bersh, P.J. 1952. Conditioned heart rate response in human beings during experimental anxiety. *Journal of Comparative and Physiological Psychology* 45:1-8.

Rachman, S. 1961. Sexual disorders and behavior

therapy. *American Journal of Psychiatry* 118:235-240.

Schachter, S.S. 1964. The interaction of co nitive and physiological determinants of emotional state. *In* L. Berkowitz (ed.), *Advances in Experimental Social Psychology,* Vol. 1. New York: Academic Press.

Silverman, R.E. 1960. Eliminating a conditioned GSR by reduction of experimental anxiety. *Journal of Experimental Psychology* 59:122-125.

Valins, S., and Ray, Alice A. 1967. Effects of cognitive desensitization on avoidance behavior. *Journal of Personality and Social Psychology* 7:345-350.

Wickens, D.D., Allen, C.K., and Hill, F.A. 1963. Effects of instructions and UCS strength on extinction of the conditioned GSR. *Journal of Experimental Psychology* 66:235-240.

6

Harvey London and
Lenore Monello

Cognitive Manipulation of Boredom

An experiment tested the effect of cognitions about time passage on feelings of boredom. Subjects were led to believe by a rigged clock that a task, actually lasting twenty physical minutes, lasted either ten minutes or thirty minutes. It was predicted that Ss in the "ten minute" condition would become more bored by the task, given that, from the Ss' point of view, time passed more slowly in this condition than in the "thirty minute" condition. The prediction was confirmed by responses on a postexperimental questionnaire, thereby extending Schachter's (1964, 1967) hypothesis concerning "cognitive labeling" of bodily states.

The work of Schachter and his colleagues (e.g., Schachter, 1964, 1967; Schachter and Latané, 1964; Nisbett and Schachter, 1966; Valins, 1966) has indicated that *S*s "label" their feelings partly in terms of the cognitions available to them. Nisbett and Schachter, for instance, have shown that a shock is less painful when *S*s attribute shock-produced autonomic symptoms to a pill. And Valins has shown that manipulating information concerning own heart rate will affect subjective evaluations of pictures of nudes.

There have been several studies suggesting that the rate at which time seems to pass is affected by one's position on the boredom/interest continuum (Geiwitz, 1964; Kerr and Keil, 1963; Loehlin, 1959; Treisman, 1963). One notices, in these studies, a tendency to focus upon psychological time as the dependent variable. But Schachter's work indicates that the relationship might be turned around, and that one might study the effect of psychological time on boredom. We became intrigued with the possibility of manipulating time by means of a rigged clock and showing a consequent change in *S*'s interest in a task.[1]

Suppose *S*s perform a task lasting 20 physical minutes. Suppose that one-half of the *S*s are led to believe by a rigged clock that the task lasted 10 minutes while the other half believe that the task lasted 30 minutes. How will such cognitions about time affect feelings of boredom?

We may outline a prediction using terminology we have found useful in dealing with psychological time (Arons and London, 1969). T_c is defined as the amount of time the *clock* indicates has passed, T_f is defined as the amount of time *felt* to have passed, and rate of time passage is then defined as T_c/T_f. Insofar as *S*s judge T_c on the basis of the rigged clock, T_c equals 10 or 30, depending on experimental condition. If *S*s are drawn from a relatively homogeneous population and randomly assigned to the two conditions, we may assume that mean T_f of *S*s in the 10-minute condition will approximately equal mean T_f of *S*s in the 30-minute condition. The simplest numerical assumption is that mean T_f within each condition = 20, since T_f, "the amount of time felt to have passed," will probably tend to average around the amount of physical time which actually passed. Thus, the rate at which time seems to pass within the 10-minute condition = 0.5 (10/20) clock minutes per felt minute and, within the 30-minute condition, 1.5 (30/20) clock minutes per felt minute. The common notion of the boredom/time relationship, that time passes slowly when one is bored, suggests that *S*s in the 10-minute condition will be relatively bored by the task, while *S*s in the 30-minute condition will be relatively interested.

METHOD

Overview

The *S* was told that the experiment would be on the physiology of moods and that it would last, all told, about an hour. Upon arrival at the psychology laboratory, *S*s were given the task of writing brief stories about each of a series of TAT pictures while a polygraph ostensibly recorded galvanic skin response. Upon completion of the task, which lasted 20 physical minutes, *E* administered a postexperimental questionnaire.

Subjects

The subjects were 32 high school and college-age males. They were paid volunteers.

Manipulation of T_C

When *S* entered the psychological laboratory, he noted an ordinary electric clock on the wall directly above the table at which he was to work. In the course of his instructions, *E* asked *S* to write down the time at the beginning of each TAT story *S* was to write so that *E* could later synchronize physiological measurements and stories. It was necessary for *S* to refer to the wall clock to carry out *E*'s request. The *E* had taken away *S*'s watch because polygraph electrodes were to be attached to *S*'s watch hand and the watch "might interfere with polygraph measurements, and the polygraph might present a hazard to the watch." *S*s were told to write stories about the pictures which lay in a pile before them on the table. They were asked to write steadily but not to worry about writing stories for all pictures, and were told that there would later be a questionnaire to fill out. A very few *S*s asked how much time they would have for the task. They were told simply that there would be "enough time."

After giving *S* instructions and attaching electrodes, *E* returned to the control room and drew out of an envelope a slip which assigned *S* to the 10-minute or the 30-minute condition. In the 10-minute condition, *E* routed the wire from the laboratory clock through equipment which made it run one-half of its normal speed so that, after the 20-minute experimental session was completed, the laboratory clock indicated that 10 minutes had passed. In the 30-minute condition, the laboratory clock was routed through equipment which made it run half again as fast as its normal speed, so that, after completion of the experimental session, the laboratory clock indicated the passage of 30 minutes.

Measurement of Boredom and Interest

Twenty physical minutes after *S* had begun the task, *E* re-entered the experimental room, turned off the polygraph, and asked *S* to stop but to write down the present time at the point he stopped. After collecting the material on the table and disconnecting *S* from the polygraph, *E* handed *S* a questionnaire "designed to find out more about responses to the TAT in order to help us understand better the physiological reactions." *E* then went to the polygraph, tore off the polygraph paper, and carried everything out of the room while *S* filled out the questionnaire.

The questionnaire asked a number of mock questions related to the ostensible purpose of the study as well as questions of immediate relevance to the experiment. To gauge *S*'s position on the boredom/interest continuum, two questions were asked. One question asked *S* to check whether he felt "increasingly more interested as ... (he) wrote more stories" on a ten-point scale running from "no more interested" to "extremely more interested," while the other question asked him to check whether he felt "increasingly more bored as ... (he) wrote more stories" on a similar ten-point scale.

In addition, the last third of the *S*s in the study answered a final, open-ended question about feelings symptomatic of boredom or interest.

While *S* filled out the questionnaire, *E* returned to the control room, turned off the clock, and plugged it back into a normal outlet.

When *S* had finished the questionnaire, *E* returned, took the questionnaire, paid *S*, returned his watch, explained the experiment, and thanked *S* for his participation.

RESULTS

Effectiveness of Manipulation

In order to be effective, the manipulation of rate of time passage must be adequately accepted and accurately perceived. With respect to acceptance, one of the 32 *S*s in the study guessed the deception and his data were therefore discarded. This rate of loss is similar to that experienced by other investigators who, with a variety of purposes, have worked with rigged clocks (cf. Craik and Sarbin, 1963; McGrath and O'Hanlon, 1967; Rotter, 1965; Schachter and Gross, 1968),

With respect to accuracy of perception, *S*s were asked on the postexperimental questionnaire how fast or slow the time seemed to pass while they were writing stories. Responses were to be indicated on a scale running from "extremely slowly" (0) to "extremely quickly" (10). *S*s in the 10-minute condition had a mean response of 3.88; *S*s in the 30-minute condition had a mean response of 8.97. The difference between these means is significant by a two-tailed t test ($p < .001$). Time did pass more quickly for *S*s in the 30-minute condition.

Effect of Rate on Boredom and Interest

We have derived that *S*s in the 30-minute condition will feel themselves to be relatively closer to the interest "end" of the boredom/interest continuum than will *S*s in the 10-minute condition. This prediction may be evaluated by constructing an interest index for each *S*. A relatively sensitive measure may be derived by simply subtracting the value of the point *S* checked on the boredom scale from the point checked on the interest scale.[2] The larger the positive value of the interest index, the more interested did *S* become in writing stories. *S*s in the 30-minute condition had a mean interest index of 4.13; *S*s in the 10-minute condition had a mean interest index of 1.56. A two-tailed t test of the difference between these means is significant ($p < .05$).

As mentioned earlier, we asked the last third of the *S*s a final, open-ended question about feelings of boredom or interest. This question asked whether either of these feelings manifested themselves as the experiment went on and, if so, how. Subjects in the 10-minute condition wrote answers such as, "I was bored because I knew what each ... (picture) was ...," and "I was mildly bored at first and felt the same as time went on," while *S*s in the 30-minute condition "became engrossed," "found it stimulating," "became absorbed." These answers indicate that the numerical ratings of boredom and interest were not mere cognitive judgments, but tended to reflect the way *S*s truly felt. Subjects for whom time passed quickly were more interested in the story-writing task than *S*s for whom time passed slowly.

DISCUSSION

The results of the reported experiment extend Schachter's notion about cognitive labeling of emotions to the state of boredom and show that this state may be influenced by altering *S*s' cognitions about the rate at which time seems to be passing. In the present study these cognitions were altered by manipulating T_c while holding T_f constant. Hoagland's (1933) hypothesized "internal clock," according to which time passes more slowly as an internal pacemaker emits more signals per unit physical time, suggests that T_f might be manipulated physiologically, and that *S*s whose "pacemakers" are made to run more quickly would find time to pass more slowly, and thus be more bored than control *S*s. Pfaff (1968) has in fact found a negative correlation between normal variation in body temperature and rate of time passage (i.e., the higher the temperature, the slower the rate), and interprets this relationship in terms of Hoagland's notion. Whether an internal pacemaker affects boredom might be a logical next question to ask.

As a side issue to the central thrust of this study, the results support the common notion of the boredom/time relationship, and accord with evidence previously presented by Loehlin (1959) and Geiwitz (1964). The contrary view, that time passes quickly when one is bored, has been suggested by both Treisman (1963) and Kerr and Keil (1963). However, Treisman's evidence that *S*s were bored seems to be based only upon his informal impression, while Kerr and Keil's article is thoroughly ambiguous in regard to the operational definition of their concept of "time drag."

As a final point, we may note that there is every reason to expect limits on the cognitive determination of bodily conditions. Schachter (1964:79) has suggested this, and Nisbett and Schachter (1966) have provided evidence for a limiting condition on the cognitive manipulation of pain. Thus, one is not surprised to find that Rotter (1965), in an experiment similar to ours, failed to obtain significant results. Rotter suggests that he failed because the task he chose--reading--was too "firmly rooted in experience ... (for) a relatively weak variable such as time rate ... (to) make any significant inroads into the *S*s' evaluations" (Rotter, 1965:52). We have used a less common task--writing stories--and have obtained significant results. Our findings thus confirm Rotter's interpretation.

NOTES

1. The research reported in this chapter was supported in part by a U.S. Public Health Service Grant. The authors would like to thank Herbert Greenwald and Irving Wolf, who allowed us to use Boston University's facilities, and Reuben Silver, who designed the apparatus for varying clock speed. The authors are grateful also to J. Stacy Adams, Richard Nisbett, Ralph Schloming, and Stuart Valins for their valuable suggestions.

2. This prodedure for combining the data from two emotion scales to produce a single index was suggested by Schachter and Singer (1962:389). It should be noted that the two components of the index each yield results completely consistent with those obtained by the use of the index.

REFERENCES

Arons, M., and London, H. 1969. Correcting for compensation in time estimation studies. *Psychonomic Science* 17:319-320.

Craik, K.H., and Sarbin, T.R. 1963. Effect of covert alterations of clock rate upon time estimates and personal tempo. *Perceptual and Motor Skills* 16:597-610.

Geiwitz, P.J. 1964. Hypnotically induced boredom and

time estimation. *Psychonomic Science* 1:277-278.

Hoagland, H. 1933. The physiological control of judgments of duration: Evidence for a chemical clock. *The Journal of General Psychology* 9:267-287.

Kerr, W.A., and Keil, R.C. 1963. A theory and factory experiment on the time-drag concept of boredom. *Journal of Applied Psychology* 47:7-9.

Loehlin, J.C. 1959. The influence of different activities on the apparent length of time. *Psychological Monographs* 73:4, Whole No. 474.

McGrath, J.J., and O'Hanlon, J. 1967. Temporal orientation and vigilance performance. *In* A.F. Sanders (ec.), *Attention and performance*. Amsterdam: North-Holland Publishing Company.

Nisbett, R.E., and Schachter, S. 1966. The cognitive manipulation of pain. *Journal of Experimental Social Psychology* 2:227-236.

Pfaff, D. 1968. Effects of temperature and time of day on time judgments. *Journal of Experimental Psychology* 76:419-422.

Rotter, G.S. 1965. Time rate as an independent variable in research. *Proceedings of the 73rd Annual Convention of the American Psychological Association:* 51-52.

Schachter, S. 1964. The interaction of cognitive and physiological determinants of emotional state. *In* L. Berkowitz (ed.), *Advances in Experimental Social Psychology,* Vol. I. New York: Academic Press.

----. 1967. Cognitive effects on bodily functioning: Studies of obesity and eating. *In* D. Glass (ed.), *Biology and Behavior: Neurophysiology and Emotion*. New York: The Rockefeller University Press and Russell Sage Foundation.

Schachter, S., and Gross, L. 1968. Manipulated time and eating behavior. *Journal of Personality and Social Psychology* 10:98-106.

Schachter, S., and Latané, B. 1964. Crime, cognition, and the autonomic nervous system. *In* D. Levine (ed.), *Nebraska Symposium on Motivation,* Vol 12. Lincoln: University of Nebraska Press.

Schachter, S., and Singer, J. 1962. Cognitive, social, and physiological determinants of emotional state. *Psychological Review* 69:379-399.

Treisman, M. 1963. Temporal discrimination and the

indifference interval: Implications for a model of the "internal clock." *Psychological Monographs* 77: 13, Whole No. 576.

Valins, S. 1966. Cognitive effects of false heartrate feedback. *Journal of Personality and Social Psychology* 4:400-408.

III

Evaluative Needs

7

Brendan Maher

Delusional Thinking and Cognitive Disorder

A hypothesis is presented regarding the genesis of paranoid delusion that attempts to take into account certain data. The data of interest are (a) the failure to find evidence of cognitive impairment in diagnosed paranoid patients, (b) the evidence of perceptual disorder as a primary and prior condition in the natural history of the clinical development of delusions and the empirical relationship of the perceptual disorder to presence of "thought disorder," (c) the failure to find evidence supporting universal psychodynamic patterns of etiology, (d) appearance of "delusional" phenomena in normal subjects in situations of deviant sensory experience, and (e) the reports of articulate patients writing of their experiences.

This hypothesis suggests that there exists a group of patients who suffer from primary perceptual anomalies, fundamentally biological in nature although probably fluctuating with current stresses, and that these anomalies involve vivid and intense sensory input. These experiences demand explanation which the patient develops through the same cognitive mechanisms that are found in normal and scientific theory-building. As the data that are available to the patient are crucially different from those available to

> *an observer, the latter judges the explanation to be bizarre and pathological. Being unable to check the validity of the patient's descriptions of his sensory experience the assumption is made that the patient is having the same experience as the observer but is defective in reality-testing and/or inferential thinking. As the evidence for the presence of perceptual disorder is stronger than the direct evidence for cognitive impairment, the hypothesis outlined here places central importance on the former. In brief, it is suggested that for many paranoid patients the delusion should be seen as the reaction of a normal, "sane" individual to abnormal but genuine perceptual experiences.*

Paranoid delusions have been generally regarded as a consequence of an underlying disorder of thinking on the part of the patient. The paranoid individual is assumed to suffer from an inability to make reasonable inferences from data. As Bandura puts it (1968:336), a delusion is a belief held in the face of evidence normally sufficient to destroy it. The presumption is that the evidence is available to the patient and that he persists in his belief in spite of it. A traditionally preferred explanation of this persistence is that there is some dysfunction in the process whereby inferences are drawn from evidence.

Research into this problem has tended to concentrate on one or other of two levels of explanation. One of them is essentially descriptive and is exemplified by the position of Von Domarus (1944) and its elaboration by Arieti (1955). This approach seeks to establish a systematic description of the delusional thought process, e.g., as a case of faulty syllogistic reasoning but leaves the problem of etiology untouched.

A second approach seeks to explain the delusional phenomena (however they have been described) in terms of some causative process. Perhaps the best known of these is the explanation in terms of underlying sexual conflict advance by Freud in the context of the case of Daniel Schreber (Freud, 1958). Here the explanation rests upon the assumption that some inner motivational state disrupts the process of logical reasoning. The delusion is at once both an instance of a general regression to primitive modes of psychological functioning and an example of a defense against complete consciousness of the underlying conflict. This position has also been elaborated by Arieti (1955, 1967) although with less emphasis upon the sexuality of the underlying conflict.

Little attention has been given to another major alternative approach, namely that the processes of inference are intact but that impairment of function in sensory input channels has distorted the evidence available to the patient's observation.[1] In the light of this possibility the delusional belief is not being held "in the face of evidence normally sufficient to destroy it," but is being held because of evidence powerful enough to support it. Where the patient may differ from a normal observer is not in the manner of drawing inference from evidence but in the kinds of perceptual experience that provide the evidence from which the inference is to be drawn. As a normal observer has no way to examine the patient's experience directly, he commonly assumes that it is the same as his own. From his assumption there is no alternative but to conclude that the patient's strange inferences are the consequences of faulty thinking. The purpose of this chapter is to develop the implications of an hypothesis that many paranoid patients suffer not from a thinking disorder but from a perceptual disorder.[2]

Before going further it is essential to emphasize that individuals diagnosed as paranoid are undoubtedly of heterogeneous origin, as is almost certainly the case with the schizophrenias generally. Some "paranoids," for example, have reasons in reality for their "delusions." What follows here refers to a hypothesized group of patients and does not presume to include all delusional patients.

EVIDENCE OF THOUGHT DISORDER

The hypothesis that a patient suffers from a thought disorder requires testing under conditions wherein the evidence presented to delusional and normal subjects is controlled, and where the range of correct inferences that might be drawn from it is very limited. It is very difficult to satisfy these requirements through clinical observation, but there are pertinent data from experimental investigations. Nims (1959), Gottesman and Chapman (1960), and Williams (1964) have studied the susceptibility of schizophrenic patients to logical error of the Von Domarus type. When adequate controls for variables such as education, verbal knowledge, etc. are introduced, there is no basis in evidence for the belief that schizophrenic patients differ from normals in their vulnerability to this type of error. Not all types of logical error are equally common in any population. The error (that of the "excluded middle") described in Von Domarus's principle is one of the more usual kind, but cannot be shown to occur more frequently in schizophrenic patients than in normals.

However, the Von Domarus principle was not developed on the basis of observations of the step-by-step reasoning processes of schizophrenic patients but by inference about the kinds of reasoning that might produce conclusions that are at odds with the evidence. It might be argued that the experimental evidence just cited is insufficient to counter the established fact that many paranoid patients do utter statements of belief that are contrary to evident fact. We can make the distinction clear by examining the application of a syllogistic reasoning model to an abstract and then to a concrete syllogism. Presented with two premises as follows, "All *a* is *b*," "All *c* is *b*," it would be incorrect to accept the conclusion that "All *a* is *c*." However, as the syllogism deals only with symbols, our judgment that the conclusion is incorrect is based exclusively upon an examination of the manner in which it corresponds to formal rules: there is no empirical test that can refute the conclusion as its terms have no empirical referents. Casting the same syllogism in concrete form we might state, "All mice are animals," "All horses are animals," and then accept the faulty conclusion that "All mice are horses." Here we have not only the test of formal correspondence with rules but also the empirical test that the operational criteria defining mice differ from those defining horses.

An individual who accepts an invalid conclusion to an abstract syllogism may be regarded as a poor student of formal logic; an individual who believes that mice are horses may be regarded as suffering from thought disorder. The reason for this discrimination is quite clear: we question the normalcy of the latter individual not because of the seeming deficiency of his logic but because of the seeming deficiencies of his observation of the environment. Thus, the strongly negative character of the experimental evidence that has been accumulated relevant to the Von Domarus principle is not all surprising: clinical observations of the kind that gave rise to this principle can be seen most parsimoniously as indicating a disorder of perception of the environment rather than a cognitive disability.

EVIDENCE OF PERCEPTUAL DISORDER

There is a rapidly increasing body of evidence to indicate that a considerable number of schizophrenic patients suffer from a disorder in the gating of sensory input. The data have been reviewed extensively by Venables (1964) and (in line with previous formulations by Payne, 1962) led him to conclude that the acute schizophrenic patient suffers from an excessively broad attention span. Under these conditions the individual finds it difficult to confine attention to one specific stimulus configuration, a circumstance that might also be described as a failure of sensory inhibition of irrelevant input. As the empirical data supporting this view are numerous and have been dealt with comprehensively by Venables, it is unnecessary to reiterate them here. Phenomenological descriptions of the patient's experiences have been provided by McGhie and Chapman (1961), in which the central characteristics of a patient's perceptions are vividness and clarity of all input with a consequent confusion whereby "figure" is indistinguishable from "ground."

The clinical validity of these phenomena is not a matter of particular dispute. Traditional psychodynamic explanations have included reference to these "symptoms" but have explained them as the sequelae of a process of psychotic transformation of the psychological functioning of the patient from a secondary to a primary mode (e.g., Arieti, 1967). In this sense the perceptual changes are assumed to be on the order of projections determined by the psychodynamics of the patient's state.

There is also general agreement that these alterations of perception are to be found early in the onset of schizophrenia (Arieti, 1955; Venables, 1964; McGhie and Chapman, 1961; Fish, 1961). We should note here that the onset of a behavior disorder means, operationally, the point at which the behavior of an individual becomes a matter of concern. It would be more correct to state that the perceptual disorders seem to occur early in the sequence of appearance of other psychotic symptoms rather than that they necessarily represent a true origin of the psychotic process. Presumably the etiological chain begins much earlier and consists of either biological or environmental events or a combination of both, having the effect of predisposing the patient to the ultimate psychosis. Although chronological priority does not, of course, confer etiological primacy upon an event, it is congruent with the hypothesis of primacy. From this point of view there is a *prima facie* reason to suppose that the perceptual disorder may be causative of the apparent thinking disorder. Overinclusion, the tendency to include irrelevant items in a concept formation task, has been studied by Payne, Matussek, and George (1959), and their data have led them to conclude that this kind of response is due to a breakdown in attentional focusing. This breakdown is conceived as a deficiency in a filter mechanism that would normally make it possible to exclude irrelevancies in a concept-formation task requiring selective attention to critical stimulus aspects. In other words, they point to the same perceptual flooding that has been described earlier in this chapter. Of particular interest is their observation that this condition is found most often in acute schizophrenics and only in chronic schizophrenics when the latter have delusions (Payne and Friedlander, 1962; Payne, 1962), further supporting the hypothesis that perceptual disorder and delusional thinking have an intimate etiological link.

THE DEVELOPMENT OF DELUSIONS

There is general clinical agreement that the development of a coherent delusional system follows a certain approximate sequence. Typically the patient's initial beliefs may be compartmentalized and fragmentary with a considerable sensory element in their content. Freud pointed out that in the case of Daniel Schreber his first "delusion" was a complaint of bodily sensations which ultimately led him to conclude that his body was undergoing some sort of biological change. Other patients may complain of unpleasant odors, of bodily pains, or distressing skin sensations. Distal perception may be involved so that descriptions are available of increased vividness of colors or difficulty in attending selectively to an auditory stimulus against background noise because of the increased prominence of the latter. We should note here that the patient is not presenting a delusion in any technical sense: he is describing an experience. The experience may be one that a normal observer has never had and hence it may appear to be deviant or bizarre. However, it cannot be defined as a delusion in the conventional sense because the observer has no proper "contrary evidence" against which to evaluate the belief.[3]

Not all of these experiences are necessarily distressing, and it is possible that when they are experienced as pleasurable, the outcome is not schizophrenia but the development of religious explanations. These experiences are important to the patient because they appear to be invested with unusual significance. This significance may be understood in terms of two factors. The first of these is the inevitable significance of any striking change in patterns of perceptual experience. Something unusual is happening to the individual in a manner that pervades large areas of his experience and that seems not to be shared by other people around him. Second, is the rather elementary psychological principle that the intensity of a stimulus will influence the perception of its significance. Ordinarily the processes of figure and ground relationships reflect the significant and the insignificant in a total perceptual field. What will be the figure and what will be ground are determined by external variables such as motivational states, past experience, and the like, together with variations in stimulus intensity in the perceptual environment itself. However, we are dealing here with patients for whom everything is "figure" and hence significant, but where there are no additional clues from motivational states as to what the significance is. Thus, the patient is faced with an environment that is at once both significant and mysterious. More correctly, we might expect the patient to be confused by the flood of stimulation but impressed with the significance of various discrete stimuli as they gain momentary control of his attentional focus.

Strange events, felt to be significant, demand explanation. It is the core of the present hypothesis that the explanations (i.e., the delusions) of the patient are derived by cognitive activity that is essentially indistinguishable from that employed by non-patients, by scientists, and by people generally. The structural coherence and internal consistency of the explanation will be a reflection of the intelligence of the individual patient. The content of the explanation will reflect the cultural experience of the patient with general explanatory systems (scientific, religious, political, etc.). In brief, then, a delusion is a hypothesis designed to explain unusual perceptual phenomena and developed through the operation of normal cognitive processes.

Because of the nature of the events that are to be explained, the delusions of different patients frequently have certain features in common. These features center on specific questions. What is happening? By what agency is it being made to happen? Why is it happening to me and not to others? All of these questions arise for the patient in the context of experience that has a quality of unusual intensity and significance and where the possibility of tolerating ambiguity by suspending explanation is therefore very much attenuated. The anxieties that are generated by any uncertainty in relation to one's own state are enormously exacerbated by the overwhelming nature of the events that must be explained. When a coherent explanation is ultimately developed, it should be accompanied by a strong feeling of personal relief together with the excitement that is produced by an intellectual insight such as one made in the laboratory or in the study. These elements might be expected to be found even if the explanation is intrinsically threatening to the patient; the kind of relief associated with "Now I know the worst," may temper the ominous implications of the explanation itself.

Answers to these questions must take into account certain experiential data. The fact that other people do not seem to share these experiences raises the possibility that either they are lying or the patient is truly an extraordinary person selected to have experiences denied to others. Although the outcome is far from dichotomous, we might suggest that when the patient concludes that other people are lying, he feels victimized and persecuted; when he concludes that other people really do not share these experiences, he feels superior to them and grandiosity results. We see the latter kind of effect very clearly, for example, the attitude of many hallucinogenic-drug users towards those who have not shared their experience.

Where the sensations are painful or unpleasant there arises the problem of identifying a causative agent. As no external causative agent is visible to the patient, then he is left with the possibility of invisible agencies. Inevitably, the concepts of popular science and religion are available to fill the gap. Radio waves, cosmic rays, ESP, hypnotism, electricity, demonaic or divine power are frequent candidates for this purpose because they possess the necessary attributes of invisibility, powerfulness, and general acceptance in the culture from which the patient comes. Political machination by powerful ubiquitous groups believed to have skill in concealment are also common elements of delusional explanations: the FBI, the Communist Party, the Catholic Church are among the favorites. This kind of theory meets the requirement of explaining the invisibility of the agent (he is disguised), but makes it necessary to look for him behind the disguise. Thus physicians, nurses, and other patients may be hypothesized as members of the agent group. Here again it is important to reiterate that these common hypotheses are rational, *given the intensity of the experiences that they are developed to explain.*

When the patient has identified the nature of his experiences and has explained both the reason for their personal uniqueness and the manner in which they are being produced, the final problem is to understand why this is happening at all. Here, the earlier history of the patient may become most evident. If the patient has a guilty secret in his past or present life, he may conclude that this explains why he is now being punished in this terrible way. Should the guilty secret be homosexuality, as Freud hypothesized in the Schreber case, then the delusion will be heavily tinged with explanations in these terms. Should there be no guilty secret of any substance, then the patient may be compelled to hypothesize punishment for some relatively minor peccadillo--an element in his explanation that will impress the observer even more with the apparent irrationality of the patient's belief system. Conversely, a grandiose explanation may involve feelings of self-esteem for past achievements or present attributes. The explanation may not involve self-esteem or self-blame, but may emphasize old enmities where the blame is ascribed to the enemy and not to the self. The number of possible explanations is limited only by the number of possible life histories that human beings might have. The commonness of certain kinds of explanations points to the commonality of life experiences that any particular culture provides.

What is important to note here is that the life experiences are not assumed to explain why the patient is delusional. There are two questions to be asked in the study of delusions. Why does the patient have a delusion? Why does he have this particular delusion? For Freud, in the analysis of the Schreber case, the same answer applied to both questions. Schreber was delusional because he had a problem of repressed homosexuality (i.e., this particular problem is the universal genesis of paranoid delusions); his delusion centered on sexual identity for the same reason. According to the hypothesis elaborated here there are different answers to each question. The patient is delusional because he is actually experiencing perceptual input that demands an explanation. The patient presents his particular delusion with content that is drawn from his past history or present circumstances because that is the kind of explanatory material available to him. The specific past history of the patient is not responsible for the rise of his delusions except insofar as the perceptual anomalies themselves may be understood as the consequences of the operation of past stresses on a biopsychological system.

A miniature version of the whole sequence may sometimes be seen in elderly people who are becoming hard of hearing. Phenomenologically the person experiences a gradual diminution in the loudness with which other people are speaking and this readily lends itself to an interpretation that they are whispering. Given this interpretation, the next problem for the subject is to understand why they are whispering and why they deny it when taxed with it. It is perfectly natural--given the interpretation of whispering--to conclude that an attempt is being made to conceal something from the listener. Thus a delusion of conspiracy is not only possible but eminently reasonable. Once this inference has been made, the chief remaining question is to understand what the object of the conspiracy is. Here, the past history of the subject becomes of great importance. If the individual has been authoritarian and punitive with his family, he may decide that they are planning revenge; if he is ashamed of some past or present activity of his own, he may conclude that it has been discovered; if he has exercised close control over the finances of the family, he may fear that there is a plot to deprive him of his money, and so on. What is of central importance to this rather simple situation is that the past history of the patient has not produced the delusion; the impairment of hearing has produced the delusion. Past history has merely helped to determine what the content of the delusion will be. The cure of the delusion is a hearing aid or a proper preliminary diagnosis of deafness. Psychotherapy directed at the content of the delusion may affect the patient's view of his own life history, but cannot eliminate the perception that other people are whispering, unless it is coupled with a recognition on the part of the patient that the trouble is an error of perception and does not lie in the external environment.

By the same token, the treatment of the paranoid schizophrenic may be seen to rest on certain propositions. The first is that while it would be ideally necessary to eliminate the primary perceptual difficulty in order to remove the conditions that compel delusions, this is not currently possible in any complete fashion. Given that we cannot yet do this, the major emphasis would be placed upon convincing the patient that the changes are in his perceptual functioning and not in the external environment. This means getting the patient to regard himself as deficient or anomalous and helping him to learn to predict and avoid those situations in which perceptual anomalies are most likely to be distressing (large crowds, noisy and visually complex environments, etc.).

Psychologically the problem has many similarities to that involved in teaching a cardiac patient to avoid sudden exercise or stresses and how to recognize warning signs when he is developing cardiac difficulties. Clearly the therapeutic goal is to enable the patient to control the consequences of his difficulties via insight into their biological nature. Emphasis upon distressing events in the patient's past life may well accentuate stress and be countertherapeutic. Certainly the well-documented inefficacy of psychodynamically oriented therapies in schizophrenia suggests the irrelevance of dynamic explanations of etiology.

Some additional implications of this general hypothesis should be mentioned briefly here. In the event that a patient has suffered from these anomalies from very early life there is a diminished necessity for him to explain them--they are, for him, normal and require no explanation. Thus, very early development of these difficulties may lead to gradual withdrawal from stimulation but not necessarily the appearance of delusions. Reactive schizophrenia consequent on unusual stress should be accompanied by a relatively brief period of perceptual anomalies and hence increased possibility that the patient will develop insight into their pathological character and fail to develop systematic delusions. The development of systematic delusions up to the point that the patient has experienced the feeling of relief mentioned earlier increases the probability that they will persist. As in science, a coherent theory is only overthrown by a better theory, and the chances that this can be done successfully by a clinician are reduced when the patient has found a generally satisfactory theory of his own. However, because the patient's theory is, in a scientific sense, invalid, it is inevitable that it will b contradicted from time to time by particular kinds of data In order to handle this, the theory must become more and more elaborate and encompassing. Thus we find that delusi al explanations tend to spread in their comprehensiveness with the passage of time.

The quality of any explanation is heavily influenced by the intelligence of the explainer. Generally speaking the test intelligence of paranoid schizophrenic patients is higher than that of other Kraepelinian subtypes of schizophrenia. Tested intelligence of hebephrenic patients is generally at the lower end of the range of schizophrenias, and we may note from the *Diagnostic and Statistical Manual of Mental Disorders* (1968) that the diagnostic criteria for the application of this label emphasize "delusions often of a somatic nature" indicating the general failure of the individual to develop the kind of coherent theory that would lead his diagnosis to be elevated to that of paranoid schizophrenia. Hence, to the extent that the quality of a delusion influences the choice of diagnostic label, the intelligence of the patient will be a significant determinant of his clinical classification.

Consideration of this hypothesis may generate the criticism that it is the readiness of the patient to consider unlikely explanations of his perceptual experiences that constitutes the core of the paranoid development. Were he of normal personality, this argument might run, then these perceptual phenomena would be recognized for what they are and there would be no delusion. In a most fundamental form, the argument can be seen in Nathan (1967) as follows:

> Every reader of this book could probably cite a number of examples of perceptual misinterpretation from his own recent behavior. What distinguishes such "normal" illusional behavior from psychopathological behavior of similar form is that when it matters, the normal person will usually take steps to check the reality of his perception and will be open to change when reality-testing behavior establishes the invalidity of his original misinterpretation of environmental cues. (Nathan, 1967:94)

According to the hypothesis presented in this chapter, the sensory quality of the experiences differs in vividness and intensity from the kinds of stimuli involved in normal misperception, and as the experiences are likely to be prolonged over considerable periods of time the machinery for reality-testing is itself impaired. In fact, when reality-testing consists in taking a closer look at the environment, it will serve to validate rather than refute the experience of the patient.

ANALOGS IN NORMAL EXPERIENCE

For obvious reasons it is difficult to test this hypothesis by direct experimentation. However, certain kinds of data can be adduced that bear on it. One line of inquiry has to do with the readiness of normal subjects to offer "delusional" explanations for their own unusual perceptual experiences. Such data comes, in the main, from investigations employing special environmental conditions (such as sensory deprivations) or hallucinogenic drugs. In both cases the subject knows beforehand that he is about to enter an unusual situation and hence is forearmed with a scientific explanation of what he is about to experience. Nevertheless, there is a growing literature reporting the development of delusional thinking in normal subjects who have taken LSD (e.g., Salvatore and Hyde, 1956; Bowers and Freedman, 1969) even after the acute effects of the drug have subsided. Jones (1966), describing experiments on sensory deprivation in normal males, reports incidents in which minor details in the setting of a meal tray produced paranoid reactions. In one case the mistaken inclusion of celery sticks in lieu of promised carrot sticks led the subject to be puzzled and then, having thought about it at length, he "finally concluded that the experimenter was trying to communicate to him that he had been selecting the stimulus series incorrectly." (Jones, 1966:293). Three other subjects responded in similar manner to inadvertent and trivial changes in the feeding arrangements. The more recent literature on the effects of sensory deprivation (Zubek, Sansom, and Phrsiazniuk, 1960; Zubek et al., 1962; Jones, 1966), has disconfirmed the earlier suggestions of Bexton, Heron and Scott (1954) that impairment of cognitive functioning was produced by this kind of environment. Hence it seems most parsimonious to conclude that the thinking of these subjects is not different from that to be found in their nonexperimental environment but represents the reactions of normal people, thinking normally[4] in the presence of an unusual sensory situation that has been prolonged for some time.

REPORTS BY PATIENTS

Among the more questionable bequests of the psychodynamic approach to psychopathology is the working assumption that the statements of the patients always require interpretation before they can be properly understood. The principle of parsimony would seem to demand that the implications of accepting the patient's reports of his experience should be exhausted and found fruitless before turning to interpretive theoretical formulations. The literature of patient experience includes reports by articulate people describing their experiences in straightforward terms. Schreber (1955) described his own auditory experiences as follows:

> During several nights when I could not get to sleep, a recurrent crackling noise in the wall of our bedroom became noticeable at shorter or longer intervals: time and again it woke me as I was about to go to sleep. Naturally we thought of a mouse although it was very extraordinary that a mouse should have found its way to the first floor of such a solidly built house. But having heard similar noises innumerable times since then, and still hearing them around me every day in daytime and at night, I have come to recognize them as undoubtedly "divine miracles". (Schreber, 1955:64)

Here we see an attempt to find a natural explanation for a perceptual experience, a failure of the explanation to fir the perceptual facts, and an ultimate development of a delusional explanation. MacDonald writes:

> What I do want to explain, if I can, is the exaggerated state of awareness in which I lived before, during and after my acute illness. At first it was as if parts of my brain "awoke" which had been dormant, and I became interested in a wide assortment of people, events, places and ideas which normally would make no impression on me. Not knowing that I was ill, I made no attempt to understand what was

> happening, but felt that there was some overwhelming significance in all this, produced by God or Satan--by the time I was admitted to the hospital I had reached a state of "wakefulness" when the brilliance of light on a window-sill or the colour of blue in the sky would be so important it could make me cry. (MacDonald, 1960:175-176)

Other reports are to be found in the work of McGhie and Chapman (1961) of essentially the same kind of perceptual experience. It has been traditional to assume that the perceived importance ascribed by patients to external stimuli is a reflection of their projection of unconscious wishes and fears. Dynamic factors, it is argued, make certain kinds of stimuli important and this exaggerated importance produces effects which the patient mistakenly assigns to the stimulus. The patients' own descriptions suggest the reverse.

PSYCHODYNAMIC EXPLANATIONS AND BIOLOGY

As the hypothesis described here represents a rejection of the projective theory of delusions advanced by psychodynamically oriented theorists, it is important to note that a biologically based hypothesis accepting the reality of perceptual anomalies only gains plausibility in the light of newer knowledge about the neurological determinants of consciousness. As this knowledge is of relatively recent date, it is not surprising that explanations developed prior to it regard the phenomena of conscious experience as recalcitrant to understanding in other than purely psychological (i.e., mentalistic) terms. Although the presence of delusions in conditions of established organic origin, such as the toxic psychoses, has been known for a long time, the larger implications of this knowledge for understanding delusions generally were not vigorously pursued. The possible role of the reticular activating system in the genesis of schizophrenia has already been advanced by Fish (1961). Although his position involves sets of neurological propositions that still await adequate validation, the discussion of delusions presented here is congruent with his views and, indeed, owes much to them. Modern understanding of the biology of consciousness has changed the possible approaches to the study of abnormal states of consciousness in the same way that the work of Krafft-Ebbing on syphilis succeeded in overturning the mentalistic explanations of Bayle regarding the nature of pathology in paresis.

NOTES

1. Attention has been given to this possibility by Fish (1961), and his priority in discussing the relationship between abnormal conscious phenomena and delusions is gladly acknowledged.

2. This chapter incorporates parts of an address delivered at the Annual Meeting of the American Psychological Association, Miami Beach, 1970, with the title "The Psychology of Delusions".

3. The term "somatic delusion" sometimes used to describe these experiences is a misnomer. To regard them as delusions suggests that the observing clinician had decided that his guesses as to the nature of the patient's phenomenal experiences are more valid than the patient's own descriptions of them.

4. It should be repeated here that "thinking normally" does not mean thinking syllogistically. It means thinking in accordance with the same processes that occur in the thinking of individuals who bear no diagnosis of psychopathology.

REFERENCES

American Psychiatric Association. 1968. *Diagnostic and Statistical Manual of Mental Disorders* (Second ed.). Washington, D.C.

Arieti, S. 1955. *Interpretation of Schizophrenia*. New York: Brunner.

----. 1967. *The Intrapsychic Self*. New York: Basic Books.

Bandura, A. 1968. A social learning interpretation of psychological dysfunctions. *In* P. London and D. Rosenhahn (eds.), *Foundations of Abnormal Psychology*. New York: Holt, Rinehart & Winston.

Bexton, W.H., Heron, W., and Scott, T.H. 1954. Effects of decreased variation in the sensory environment.

Canadian Journal of Psychology 109:70-76.

Bowers, M.B., and Freedman, D. 1969. "Psychedelic" experiences in acute psychoses. *In* C. Tart (ed.), *Altered States of Consciousness.* New York: John Wiley.

Fish, F.J.A. 1961. A neuropsychological theory of schizophrenia. *Journal of Mental Science* 107:828-839.

Freud, S. 1958. Psychoanalytic notes on an autobiographical account of a case of paranoia (dementia paranoides). *In Standard Edition of the Complete Psychological Works of Sigmund Freud,* Vol. 12. London: Hogarth.

Gottesman, L., and Chapman, L.J. 1960. Syllogistic reasoning errors in schizophrenia. *Journal of Consulting Psychology* 24:250-255.

Jones, A. 1966. Information deprivation in humans. *In* B.A. Maher (ed.), *Progress in Experimental Personality Research,* Vol. III. New York: Academic Press.

MacDonald, N. 1960. Living with schizophrenia. *Canadian Medical Journal* 82:218-221; 678-681.

McGhie, A., and Chapman, J. 1961. Disorders of attention and perception in early schizophrenia. *British Journal of Medical Psychology* 24:103-116.

Nathan, P.E. 1967. *Cues, Decisions and Diagnoses: A Systems-analytic Approach to the Diagnosis of Psychopathology.* New York: Academic Press.

Nims, J.P. 1959. Logical reasoning in schizophrenia: the Von Domarus principle. Ph.D. Dissertation, University of Southern California.

Payne, R.W. 1962. An object classification test as a measure of overinclusive thinking in schizophrenic patients. *British Journal of Social and Clinical Psychology* 1:213-221.

Payne, R.W., and Friedlander, A. 1962. A short battery of simple tests for measuring overinclusive thinking. *Journal of Mental Science* 108:362-367.

Payne, R.W., Mattussek, P., and George, E.I. 1959. An experimental study of schizophrenic thought disorder. *Journal of Mental Science* 105:627-652.

Salvatore, S., and Hyde, R. 1956. Progression of effects of LSD. *Archives of Neurology and Psychiatry* 76:50-59.

Schreber, D. 1955. *Memoirs of My Nervous Illness.* Cambridge, Mass.: Robert Bentley.

Venables, P.H. 1964. Input dysfunction in schizophrenia. *In* B.A. Maher (ed.), *Progress in Experimental Personality Research,* Vol. I. New York: Academic Press.

Von Domarus, E. 1944. The specific laws of logic in schizophrenia. *In* J. Kasanin (ed.), *Language and Thought in Schizophrenia.* Berkeley: University of California Press.

Williams, E.B. 1964. Deductive reasoning in schizophrenia. *Journal of Abnormal and Social Psychology* 69: 47-61.

Zubek, J.P., Aftanas, M., Hasek, J., Sansom, W., Schuldermann, E., Wilgosh, L., and Winocur, G. 1962. Intellectual and perceptual changes during prolonged perceptual deprivation: Low illumination and noise level. *Perceptual and Motor Skills* 15:171-198.

Zubek, J.P., Sansom, W., and Phrsiazniuk, A. 1960. Intellectual changes during prolonged isolation (darkness and silence). *Canadian Journal of Psychology* 14:233-243.

IV

The Process of Explaining Internal Cues

8

John C. Barefoot and
Ronald B. Straub

Opportunity for Information Search and the Effect of False Heart Rate Feedback

The role of information search in the attribution of physiological states was investigated by manipulating the subject's opportunity for information search following the presentation of false information about his heart-rate reactions to photographs of female nudes. Consistent with the self-persuasion hypothesis proposed by Valins, the rated attractiveness of the slides was not affected by the false heart-rate feedback for those subjects who were prevented from visually searching the slides. Those subjects who had ample opportunity to view the slides rated those slides accompanied by false information of a heart-rate change as more attractive than those slides which were not paired with a change in heart rate.

Schachter and Singer (1962) have hypothesized that a state of physiological arousal for which the subject has no immediate explanation will give rise to "evaluative needs," causing the subject to actively search the environment for an appropriate explanation or "label" for his arousal. The subject's choice of an explanation wil in large part determine the nature of the subsequent

Reprinted from the *Journal of Personality and Social Psychology*, 1971, Vol. 17, No. 2, 154-157.

subjective and behavioral manifestations of the arousal. This hypothesis implies the following three component processes: (a) Unexplained arousal gives rise to subjective uncertainty and the need to reduce that uncertainty; (b) the need for uncertainty reduction results in a search for information about the nature of the arousal; and (c) the search process culminates in the choice of an explanation for the arousal, reducing uncertainty and determining the nature of the subjective experience.

The hypothesized effect of physiological arousal has been tested in experiments which directly manipulated physiological states (Schachter and Singer, 1962; Schachter and Wheeler, 1962), and the importance of the labeling process has been investigated through the manipulation of available explanations for an existing state of arousal (e.g., Nisbett and Schachter, 1967; Ross, Rodin, and Zimbardo, 1969). While these experimental approaches have assumed the presence of an intervening information-search process, relatively little direct attention has been paid to the nature of that search process. Several studies (e.g., Gerard, 1963; Gerard and Rabbie, 1961; and Schachter, 1959) have indirectly assessed the need for information in states of emotional arousal by measuring the strength of affiliative tendencies, hypothesizing that the desire to be with others reflects the need for information about one's own emotional state. As Gerard (1963) has noted, however, the affiliation measure contains components other than the need for information, and a "purer" measure is needed. The research reported in this study[1] is an attempt to examine more closely the role of information search in the process of attribution of physiological arousal.

Some ideas about the importance of information-search processes can be obtained from an article by Valins (1966), in which false information about heart rate was shown to affect subjective reactions to stimuli which had been presented concurrently with the heart-rate information. Subjects viewed slides of female nudes while listening to sounds that they believed to be their heartbeats. The sounds, actually controlled by the experimenter, changed in frequency when five of the slides were presented and remained relatively constant on the remaining five presentations. Those slides which had been paired with the change in false heart rate (reinforced) were later judged by the subjects to be more attractive than the slides which had been associated with no change in heart sounds (nonreinforced).

In his discussion of these findings, Valins hypothesized that the subject, upon hearing the change in heart rate, selectively searched the slides for attributes which might have caused such a dramatic heart-rate reaction, affecting his perception of the slides in the process. In effect, the subject convinced himself that the slide was attractive, and he invested considerable cognitive effort in this self-persuasion process. Valins based this hypothesis on the spontaneous comments of subjects and on the fact that subjects interviewed several weeks after the experiment still strongly preferred the slides which had been reinforced, suggesting that the effect was more than transitory. In addition, Valins (personal communication, 1969) attempted to attenuate the effect of the feedback by revealing the false nature of the feedback after the manipulation, but before the dependent measure was obtained. He found, however, that even when the subjects were aware of the deception, they strongly preferred the slides which had been reinforced, a finding which is consistent with the idea that the feedback initiates a process which results in a rather permanent cognitive reorganization.

The self-persuasion hypothesis is considerably more complex than the simple inferential process ("I react physiologically to the slide, therefore I like it") that could account for the available data. It also suggests that the false feedback might be ineffective in changing attitudes toward the slides if the subject were prevented from completing the process of self-persuasion.

In the experiment reported below, this hypothesis was tested by manipulating the subjects' opportunity for information search. In a modified version of Valins's heart-rate feedback situation, low-search-condition subjects were prevented from visually searching the photographs by shortening the slide exposure times, while high-search-condition subjects were provided with relatively long exposure times. It was hypothesized that unlike the high-search subjects, the low-search subjects would be unable to complete the self-persuasion process, and their attitudes toward the slides would be unaffected by the feedback.

Provided that the subjects learn the association between the slide and the false feedback, there is no reason to suppose that the necessary information search must take place simultaneously with the presentation of the feedback. If the subjects were prevented from extensively viewing the slides while they were receiving the false feedback, but were later given an opportunity to search the slides before the dependent measure was obtained, they should still be able to make the necessary cognitive reorganization and should therefore change their attitudes about the slides. A delayed-search condition was run in order to test this hypothesis.

METHOD

Subjects

Male introductory psychology students were recruited from classes at Dartmouth College for an experiment on "physiological reactions to visual stimuli," and were randomly assigned to the experimental conditions. One of the 37 subjects was eliminated from the analysis because he failed to understand the experimenter's instructions. None of the subjects reported any suspicion regarding the nature of the experimental manipulations. All received course credit for their participation.

Manipulation of Information about Heart Rate

Upon entering the experimental room, the subject was told that the experiment involved the measurement of heart-rate reactions to sexually arousing stimuli, photographs of female nudes. EKG electrodes were placed on the subject, and the nature of heart-rate recording was explained. The experimenter further explained that a measure of resting heart rate would be taken, followed by the slide presentations and another rest period. After instructing the subject to relax and answering any questions, the experimenter turned off the light, stationed himself at the polygraph, and the 2-minute initial rest period began. Following the rest period, 10 slides of female nudes from *Playboy* magazine were shown for 30 seconds apiece, with 30-second interslide intervals (Presentation 1). The order of presentation was the same for all subjects. A 2-minute rest period followed the first presentation series.

Toward the end of the second rest period, the experimenter said, "Now I am going to show you a second series, consisting of those slides which caused the greatest heart-rate reaction during the first presentation." Five slides were then shown to the subject (Presentation 2), constituting the reinforcement procedure. For half of the subjects in each condition, Slides 1, 3, 6, 8, and 9 were reinforced. Slides 2, 4, 5, 7, and 10 were shown to the remaining subjects. This counterbalancing insured that the feedback effect was independent of the intrinsic attractiveness of the photographs.

After the reinforcement procedure, the cardiac electrodes were removed, and the subject was asked to answer a questionnaire to "help us interpret your heart rate." In addition to several items about his medical history, the questionnaire asked the subject to rate the attractiveness of each of the slides. Fifty-point rating scales were provided, with the ends of the scales labeled "Not at all attractive" and "Extremely attractive." While the subject was making these ratings, the slides were shown to him again in the same order as in Presentation 1.

Manipulation of Exposure Time

In the low-search condition, subjects were given only a minimal amount of time to view the slides during the reinforcement and rating procedures, preventing extensive visual search. During Presentation 2, the reinforcement procedure, each of the five reinforced slides was shown for 5 seconds, with 25-second intervals. Identical exposure times were used during the rating procedure.

Subjects in the high-search condition viewed the five reinforced slides for 20 seconds apiece during Presentation 2, with 10-second intervals. The rating-period exposures were the same as in the low-search condition, 5 seconds apiece at 30-second intervals.

In the delayed-search condition, the Presentation 2 exposure times were equal to those in the low-search condition, 5 seconds, with 25-second interslide intervals.

Subjects in this condition, however, had the opportunity for the necessary visual search during the rating period, when the slides were presented for 20 seconds apiece with 10 seconds between slides.

The exposure-time manipulations are summarized in Table 8.1.

TABLE 8.1. Slide Exposure Times in the Three Search Conditions (In Seconds)

	Presentation		
Condition	*1*	*2*	*Rating*
Low search	30	5	5
High search	30	20	5
Delayed search	30	5	20

RESULTS

Table 8.2 presents the mean attractiveness ratings of the slides in each condition. As predicted, the ratings were affected by the feedback in the high-search and delayed search conditions, but no effect was observed in the low-search condition. The difference between reinforced and nonreinforced slides in the low-search condition was significantly smaller than the difference in the combined high-search and delayed-search conditions. The F ratio for the predicted component of the Condition X Reinforcement interaction was 4.13 ($df = 1/33$, $p = .05$).

TABLE 8.2. Mean Slide Attractiveness Ratings

	Slide		
Condition	*Reinforced*	*Nonreinforced*	*t*
Low search	29.62	29.47	.08
High search	31.32	26.00	2.29*
Delayed search	33.12	27.44	2.66*

Note: -n = 12 in each condition.
*$p < .05$.

DISCUSSION

The ratings of the low-search subjects, who only viewed the slides for a very short period of time during the feedback presentation, were not affected by the feedback. It might be suggested that the exposure-time manipulation not only affected the opportunity for information search, as was intended, but it might have made the feedback seem unimportant to the low-search subjects, or it might have made it difficult for them to remember which slides had been reinforced. The delayed-search subjects also had short exposure times during the feedback manipulation, however, and the fact that their ratings were affected by the feedback argues against this interpretation of the data.

One might also argue that subjects tend to prefer those slides with which they are most familiar. Since they viewed the reinforced slides longer than the nonreinforced slides, and since it has been hypothesized that they attend to the reinforced slides more closely than the nonreinforced slides, it follows that the subjects should be most familiar with the reinforced photographs and hence rate them as being more attractive. This line of reasoning might account for the feedback effect, not only in the delayed-search and high-search conditions, but in the Valins study as well. This process should also affect the ratings of the nonreinforced slides, however, leading to the prediction that the subjects who would most like the nonreinforced slides would be those in the delayed-search condition, since those subjects viewed the nonreinforced slides longer than the subjects in any other condition. This was not the case in the obtained results. The familiarity hypothesis, at least in its simplest form, also has difficulty in accounting for the failure to find an effect in the low-search condition.

The rating data of this experiment support the idea that the heart-rate feedback effect is mediated by a relatively complex cognitive process which involves information search. Without the opportunity for information search, the feedback was ineffective in changing the subject's attitudes. Obviously, a more detailed analysis of the mediating process is warranted. Direct measurement of the duration and intensity of information search would be essential in continued investigation of this process.

It should be noted that the feedback manipulation employed in this experiment was a considerably simplified version of the procedure used by Valins. The effectiveness of the new procedure serves to increase the generality of the Valins findings. This experiment also makes it more difficult to account for Valins's results solely in terms of demand characteristics, since the demand in the low-search condition was presumably equal to that in the other conditions.

NOTE

1. Requests for reprints should be sent to John Barefoot, Department of Psychology, Carleton University, Ottawa 1, Canada.

REFERENCES

Gerard, H.B. 1963. Emotional uncertainty and social comparison. *Journal of Abnormal and Social Psychology* 66:568-573.

Gerard, H.B., and Rabbie, J.M. 1961. Fear and social comparison. *Journal of Abnormal and Social Psychology* 62:586-592.

Nisbett, R., and Schachter, S. 1967. Cognitive manipulation of pain. *Journal of Experimental Social Psychology* 2:227-236.

Ross, L., Rodin, J., and Zimbardo, P.G. 1969. Toward an attribution therapy: The reduction of fear through induced cognitive-emotional misattribution. *Journal of Personality and Social Psychology* 12:279-288.

Schachter, S. 1959. *The Psychology of Affiliation.* Minneapolis: University of Minnesota Press.

Schachter, S., and Singer, J.E. 1962. Cognitive, social, and physiological determinants of emotional state. *Psychological Review* 69:379-399.

Schachter, S., and Wheeler, L. 1962. Epinepherine, chloropromazine, and amusement. *Journal of Abnormal*

and Social Psychology 65:121-128.
Valins, S. 1966. Cognitive effects of false heart rate feedback. *Journal of Personality and Social Psychology* 4:400-408.

9

Stuart Valins

Persistent Effects of Information about Internal Reactions: Ineffectiveness of Debriefing

A process of self-persuasion has been advanced to account for the effects of information about internal reactions on attitudes toward emotional stimuli. To determine whether the results of this cognitive activity would be resistant to debriefing, Ss *were shown slides of female nudes while hearing their alleged heart-rate reactions and were subsequently informed that these reactions were part of a deception manipulation. It was found that, although* Ss *accepted the debriefing, the false information continued to exert an influence on their attitudes toward the nudes. The attitudes of these* Ss *toward the nudes were the same as those of* Ss *who were not debriefed.*

It has been found that information about physiological reactions can influence subjective and behavioral reactions to emotional stimuli. Subjects are more apt to like slides of female nudes if led to believe that their hearts have reacted to these stimuli (Valins, 1966; 1967), and are more apt to approach a live snake if led to believe that their hearts have not reacted to snake stimuli (Valins and Ray, 1967). These effects have also been found to be relatively long-lasting. Those studies using slides of female nudes as stimuli have found the effects of the manipulations to last for periods of up to two months.

A process of self-persuasion has been advanced to account for the strength of these effects (Valins, 1966). Specifically, it has been hypothesized that subjects invest considerable cognitive activity in convincing themselves that, in accord with their presumed heart-rate reactions, a given girl is attractive or unattractive, or that a snake is not very frightening. If we assume the existence of such self-persuasion, it is reasonable that the results of this process would be relatively persistent and resistant to change.

This chapter[1] reports an attempt to modify the effects of false heart-rate feedback by subsequently neutralizing the information which initiated the self-persuasion. Subjects were shown slides of female nudes while hearing sounds that they believed were their heart beats. After seeing all of the slides they were "debriefed" (about the deceptive nature of the feedback but not about our interest in the attractiveness of the nudes) and ratings of their liking for the slides were immediately obtained. Should these ratings be different from those of *S*s who are not debriefed? If *S*s have convinced themselves that a given girl is attractive or unattractive, then it might be expected that the debriefing would have little effect. Although these *S*s realize that the slides did not have different physiological effects, it is hypothesized that this knowledge alone will not be sufficient to modify the effects of self-persuasion. It is believed that *S*s must have sufficient time to consider the implications of the debriefing and to re-evaluate the slides. To test this hypothesis, other *S*s were debriefed and left alone for ten minutes before they rated the slides. It is predicted that, in comparison to *S*s who are not debriefed, these subjects will show little, if any effect of the heart-rate feedback.

METHOD

Male undergraduates viewed slides of female nudes while hearing sounds that they thought were their heart beats, and which indicated that their hearts had reacted to some slides but not to others. At the end of this procedure, half of the *S*s were debriefed and told that the sounds were not their heart beats; the remaining *S*s were not debriefed. Half of each of these groups rated the attractiveness of the girls immediately after being debriefed or not; the remaining *S*s rated the attractiveness of the girls ten minutes after being debriefed or not.

Manipulation of Information about Internal Reactions

All *S*s were led to believe that the experimenter was interested in their heart-rate and galvanic skin responses (GSR) to slides of female nudes. GSR was presumably picked up via electrodes which were taped to their arms and recorded on a meter in an adjacent room. Heart rate was presumably picked up via a microphone taped to their chests. This microphone allegedly resulted in an audible heart sound which was tape recorded in the subject's room. The subjects were told to ignore the heart sounds.

After attaching the suitable electrodes, the experimenter started the tape recorder and left the room. Rather than recording the *S*s' heart beats, the tape recorder actually played a recording of heart-like sounds. The *S*s heard these sounds beat at a "normal" rate for two minutes. Beginning with the third minute, ten slides of female nudes were projected, at one-minute intervals, into the *S*'s room through a one-way screen. The slide presentation was coordinated with the tape recording so that *S*s heard a marked increase in the rate of the sounds to five of the slides and no change in the rate of the sounds to five different slides. After the tenth slide, all of the slides were shown again with the same "heart-rate" reactions occurring to the same slides.

The slides that were used were made from photographs published by Playboy magazine. Ten slides were divided into two sets of five which were equal in attractiveness. Half of the *S*s in each condition heard a change in their "heart-rate" to one set of slides and the remaining *S*s heard a change to the other set of slides. Between-condition comparisons are thus independent of the objective attractiveness of the slides. The effects of slide set were insignificant for all analyses.

Debriefing

After presenting the last slide, the experimenter returned and said:

Would you be very surprised if I told you that those sounds you heard were not your heart beats? They weren't. Those sounds were really regular electrical impulses that we recorded and played back to you through this speaker. This hidden wire leads directly from the tape recorder to the speaker. I was able to coordinate the slides with the recording by using my stop watch. That way, I simply presented the slides when there was a change in the frequency of the beats. The slide came on a second or two before the change. We set up the conditions so that you would hear a change in the rate to the 1st, 3rd, 6th, 8th, and 9th, slides, and no change to the others.

We are really interested in your actual heart rate reactions to what you think is your heart rate. That is, our heart beat at times becomes noticeable to us in the form of palpitations. We are trying to determine whether our awareness of our heart beat in turn affects our heart. Does our heart rate speed up or slow down when we become aware of it? By the way, the electrodes on your fingers didn't measure skin resistance. They actually pick up electrical impulses from your heart which are recorded in the next room and which enable us to determine your real heart rate. Is this clear?

We use slides of nude females just to present a stimulus which you think could reasonably affect your heart rate. That way you'd believe that the sounds were really your heart beats. You probably wouldn't believe it if the slides were of houses or unattractive females.

*No Delay S*s were then shown the slides again and rated their attractiveness using a 100-point scale. The experimenter was presumably interested in their ratings as a way of retaining only the most attractive slides for subsequent experiments. *Delay S*s were left alone for 10 minutes prior to their ratings of the slides. The experimenter had allegedly gone to obtain a post-experimental questionnaire.

No Debriefing

After presenting the last slide, the experimenter returned and briefly discussed the procedure with the *S*s. *No Delay S*s were then shown the slides again and rated their attractiveness using a 100-point scale. Again, the experimenter was presumably interested in retaining only the most attractive ones for subsequent experiments. *Delay S*s were left alone for 10 minutes prior to rating the slides.

Photograph Choices

Upon completion of the rating procedure, the experimenter answered any questions that the *S*s posed and then dismissed them. As the *S* was leaving, the experimenter said, "Oh, I almost forgot. Playboy has sent us dozens of these calendars. Rather than throw them away, Dr. Valins thought you fellows might like some. Just pick the five you like best and I'll get copies for you." The experimenter then left and subsequently returned empty-handed. He explained that he had asked the *S* to pick the photographs only to determine if the method of presentation, slide versus photograph, affected the attractiveness of certain nudes. Just before dismissing the *S*s, the experimenter debriefed the No Debrief *S*s using the same rationale as for the Debrief *S*s.

RESULTS

It was hypothesized that information about internal reactions would not be neutralized by debriefing if *S*s have little time to consider the implications of the debriefing (No Delay), but that it would be neutralized if sufficient time is available (Delay). Thus, the reinforced nudes should be liked more than the nonreinforced ones for both Debrief and No Debrief *S*s in the No Delay conditions, but liking of the nudes should be greater for the No Debrief *S*s than for the Debrief *S*s in the Delay conditions. The data required to test this hypothesis are presented in Table 9.1. It will be noted first that, combining all conditions, reinforced nudes were rated more attractive than non-reinforced ones ($t = 5.44$, $p < .001$), and more reinforced photographs than non-reinforced ones were chosen as rewards (t = 4.10, $p < .001$). It is also apparent that there is little difference between the experimental conditions on either dependent measure. Analyses of variance revealed that no effect approached significance (only one F value produced a p of $< .25$).

TABLE 9.1. Attractiveness of Reinforced Nudes Relative to Non-Reinforced Nudes.

Experiment 1

Condition	*N*	*Mean Difference in Ratings*	*Number of Reinforced Photographs Chosen*
No Debrief			
Immediate	8	+20.25	4.0
Delay	8	+15.08	3.0
Debrief			
Immediate	8	+17.28	3.1
Delay	8	+10.12	3.1

One must conclude from these data that the debriefing did not effectively overcome the information that the *S*s had been given about their internal reactions. Regardless of the time that the *S*s had to consider the implications of the debriefing for their attitudes toward the nudes, subjects from both Debrief conditions rated the reinforced nudes higher in attractiveness than the non-reinforced ones (t = 3.42, $p < .01$) and chose more of the reinforced nudes as rewards (t = 3.00, $p < .01$). Thus, we can infer that *S*s thoroughly convinced themselves that they liked or disliked certain nudes prior to the debriefing and that the effects of this self-persuasion persisted even when *S*s had time to consider that they had no physiological reason to like one girl more than another.[2]

Although the results of the Delay conditions are consistent with those of the No Delay conditions, it was originally expected that the delay would provide sufficient opportunity for the debriefing to be effective. To check these unexpected results, the Delay conditions were replicated and a control group was also added. The control *S*s underwent the identical procedure as the experimental *S*s but they knew throughout the experiment that the sounds were tape recorded (The experimenter was presumably interested in whether "extraneous sounds" would modify their GSR reactions to the slides). The relevant data are presented in Table 9.2.

TABLE 9.2. Attractiveness of Reinforced Nudes Relative to Non-Reinforced Nudes.

		Experiment 2 (all conditions with Delay)	
Condition	*N*	*Mean Difference in Ratings*	*Number of Reinforced Photographs Chosen*
Debrief	10	+19.50	3.2
No Debrief	10	+13.40	3.0
Control	10	+ .60	2.7

It can be seen that once again the debriefing was ineffective. The attractiveness ratings given by the debriefed and non-debriefed *S*s were similar. Both groups rated the reinforced nudes as more attractive than the non-reinforced ones ($t = 4.94$, $p < .001$), and this effect was greater than for the control *S*s ($t = 3.05$, $p < .01$). The photograph choices yielded similar data but none of the differences between groups approached significance.

DISCUSSION

Before pursuing the implications of these data, it is necessary to discuss an obvious alternative explanation; were debriefed *S*s convinced that they had not heard their heart-rate reactions? If debriefed *S*s did not believe the debriefing then there would be little reason for their data to be different from that of *S*s who were not debriefed. This alternative explanation is not very compelling in view of the fact that all debriefed *S*s were taken to the equipment table and shown the means by which the sounds were played rather than recorded. Furthermore, responses to a questionnaire given at the end of experiment 2 indicated that, in comparison to control *S*s, debriefed *S*s believed that the sounds were their heart beats before the debriefing ($p < .01$) but did not believe it after the debriefing (Debrief *S*s post-debriefing versus control, $p = ns$; Debrief *S*s pre-versus-post-debriefing, $p < .01$). It is thus likely that the debriefed *S*s realized that the feedback was false.

If *S*s realized that the sounds that they heard were not their heart beats, and if some *S*s had sufficient time to consider this, why were their attitudes toward the nudes still affected by the heart-rate feedback. In post-experimental interviews many subjects indicated that they did not consciously distort the nudes to bring their attractiveness estimates in line with the feedback. Rather, they thought that the false feedback brought their attention to inherently positive or negative features of the nudes. Having found these objective features, the subjects should not then be influenced by the debriefing. Debriefing and time to consider the implications of the debriefing should be irrelevant variables if subjects believe that they were not influenced by the false feedback.

This interpretation of the data implies that subjects were actively involved in validating the information conveyed by the false feedback. The subjects were not passively inferring liking or disliking from their autonomic behavior. Rather, the false feedback provided them with an hypothesis which they "tested" by scanning the various features of the nudes. One implication of this hypothesis-testing notion has been studied by Barefoot and Straub (1971). They reasoned that the false feedback should be effective only when subjects have an adequate opportunity to scan the slides of the nudes. In accord with their hypothesis, subjects who viewed the slides for 25 seconds manifested a large and significant false-feedback effect whereas subjects who viewed the slides for 10 seconds manifested no effect. The Barefoot and Straub experiment and the present experiment both suggest that false heart-rate feedback influences subjects by setting up an hypothesis. Subjects then test the hypothesis by finding objective supporting information.

NOTES

1. This research was supported in part by research Grants MH 12715 and MH 14557 from the National Institute of Mental Health. Experimental data were expertly gathered by Steven Riesman, Robert Calder, and Robert Colman.

2. An attempt was made to assess the *S*s' attitudes toward the nudes several weeks after the initial experimental session. Although these findings were generally consistent with the data reported, an insufficient number of *S*s could be contacted.

REFERENCES

Barefoot, J., and Straub, R. 1971. Opportunity for information search and the effect of false heart-rate feedback. *Journal of Personality and Social Psychology* 17:154-157.

Valins, S. 1966. Cognitive effects of false heart-rate feedback. *Journal of Personality and Social Psychology* 4:400-408.

----. 1967. Emotionality and information concerning internal reactions. *Journal of Personality and Social Psychology* 6:458-463.

Valins, S., and Ray, Alice Allen. 1967. Effects of cognitive desensitization on avoidance behavior. *Journal of Personality and Social Psychology* 7:345-350.

V

The Effects of External Cues

10

Aaron Beck

Cognition, Affect, and Psychopathology

The relationship of cognition to affect in normal subjects is similar to that observed in psychopathological states. The specific cognitive content determines the affective response. Among normals the sequence perception - cognition - emotion is dictated largely by the demand character of the stimulus situation. The appraisal of personal danger leads to anxiety; of loss, to sadness; of unwarranted infringement, to anger; of self-enhancement, to euphoria.

In psychopathological conditions, the reaction to the stimulus situation is determined to a much greater extent by internal processes. The affective response, furthermore, is likely to be excessive or inappropriate because of the idiosyncratic conceptualization of the event. The input from the external situation is molded to conform to the typical schemas activated in these conditions. As a result, interpretations of experience embody arbitrary judgments, overgeneralizations, and distortions.

A classification of neurotic conditions based on the typical cognitive content of each of the disorders is presented. Perseverative conceptualizations relevant to danger, loss, unjustified attack, and self-enhancement are typical of anxiety neuroses, depression, paranoid states, and hypomanic states, respectively. These formulations allow predictions of which emotions or psychopathological states will occur, given alternative cognitive conditions.

Despite the numerous social psychological studies investigating the relation of cognitive processes to affect, there have been relatively few studies of the relationship of these variables in psychopathological conditions. Menninger's (1963) resumé of the evolution of psychiatric classification demonstrates the historical pattern of regarding disorders of the "emotional life" as entities distinct from disorders of the "intellectual life." Traditional faculty psychology is reflected in the constructions by Bucknill and Tuke (1879) of the classes of Diseases of the Intellect, Diseases of the Emotions or Moral Sentiments, and Diseases of the Instincts or Propensities. Contemporary psychiatry has preserved the time-honored notion that, by definition, conditions such as mania and depression are primary affective disorders in which cognitive factors play a minimal or secondary role.

The peripheral position assigned to cognitive processes in affective disorders is illustaated in the *Diagnostic and Statistical Manual* of the American Psychiatric Association (1968:35). The single reference to cognitive distortions asserts that delusions in these conditions are attributable to the primary mood disorder. The official position is maintained in recent textbooks of psychiatry (Gregory, 1968; Kolb, 1968).

This notion of the primacy of affect over cognition in psychopathology presents an interesting paradox: for normal subjects, the conceptualization of a situation determines the affective state, but in psychopathology, the affective state determines the cognition. This paradox deserves closer scrutiny than it has received.

On the basis of clinical observations and subsequent research, this author has postulated that in abnormal conditions such as depression and anxiety the direction of the reaction is from cognition to affect, just as it is in normal responses (Beck, 1963). The difference between normal and abnormal reactions lies in the degree of correspondence between the conceptualization and the veridical stimulus configuration. In psychopathological states perseverative faulty conceptualization leads to excessive or inappropriate affective disturbance.

The typical conceptualizations leading to specific affects appear to be the same in both "normal" and "abnormal" responses. In abnormal conditions, however, conceptualizations are determined to a greater extent by internal processes which distort the stimulus situation.

Arnold (1960) emphasized the importance of the appraisal of an event in determining the affective response. Lazarus (1966) extended this notion by postulating primary and secondary appraisals of threatening stimuli. The initial recognition and labeling of a noxious stimulus is followed or accompanied by an assessment of the individual's counter-harm resources and coping mechanisms. The degree of mobilized anxiety is related to the balance between the threat as perceived by the individual and the degree to which he believes he can cope with the threat.

The conceptualization of a stimulus situation probably involves multiple appraisals and reappraisals of the external situation and the individual's ability to cope with it. Furthermore, the emotional response to the appraised situation also comprises part of the stimulus environment. The way the individual "reads" the feedback from these internal responses contributes further to his complex appraisal of the situation. The labeling of an internal event as anxiety, for example, may enhance the degree to which the external stimulus is regarded as dangerous.

The sequence between the initial registration of a stimulus and final closure may be formulated in terms of continuous matching of incoming perceptual data against an individual's conceptual categories (schemas). Initially, the stimulus may invoke a cognitive schema that is relatively broad and undifferentiated. Subsequently, a more specific and appropriate category may be activated. There is a progression from a crude categorization to a relatively refined categorization until the final adjustment is made between the incoming data and the cognitive schema. In psychopathological conditions, in which certain types of schemas are dominant, the adjustment between external stimulus and internal category may be poor; then the conceptualization of a stimulus situation will be determined more by the invoked schema than by the configuration of the external stimulus.

SPECIFIC CONDITIONS FOR INSTIGATION OF AFFECTS

The affects described in this chapter[1] are those most relevant to clinical disturbances. The focus will be on sadness, elation, anxiety, and anger, which are clinically important in depressive, manic, anxiety, and paranoid states, respectively.

The model for affect instigation is based on certain assumptions. First, irrespective of the veridical properties of a stimulus situation, an individual's reaction to the situation depends upon his appraisal (or conceptualization) of the situation. Crucial properties of the stimulus are its connotations, meanings, and significance for the perceiver.

Second, the cognitive content or meaning is chained to a particular affect. As the cognitive content changes, the affect changes in consonance with it. Affect-producing ideation may occur in response to a specific external stimulus or may occur in a sequence of associations in the "stream of consciousness." The affect is congruent with the cognitions.

During the course of a person's development, a particular cognitive content may establish a pathway to a specific affect. Some of these cognition-affect chains appear to be universal. Others are idiosyncratic for a particular society or a specific individual.

Third, the special significance of a particular event in terms of its presumed effect on the individual's domain is an important determinant of the affective response. The domain of an individual encompasses all the objects and attributes of those objects which have any value or significance to him. If a particular object is irrelevant, unknown, unknowable, or totally lacking in any actual or potential investment, then it is not part of the domain.

The domain, thus, consists of the individual as a physical entity, his personal attributes, and various other animate and inanimate objects in which he has an investment. Among these other objects are, typically, the individual's family, friends, material possessions. In addition are the groups or other individuals with whom he identifies himself (for example, his country, his racial group, or his school team), as well as intangible values or ideals of importance to him -- liberty, democracy, law and order, property rights.

The kinds of conceptualizations leading to the clinically relevant affects are presented in Table 10.1.

TABLE 10.1. Cognitive Content Relevant to Specific Affects and Psychopathological Disorders

Appraisal of Stimulus	*Affect*	*Psychopathological Disorder*
Loss	Sadness	Depression
Gain	Euphoria	Hypomanic State
Danger	Anxiety	Anxiety Neurosis
Offense	Anger	Paranoid State

Sadness

It is observable that a person feels sad when he experiences loss. The loss is chained to the response of sadness or dysphoria.

The special meaning of a particular loss to an individual determines the degree of emotional response. In order to produce sadness, a loss must be conceived by the person as subtracting from his domain in some significant way. For example, a wealthy person losing a few dollars may be indifferent to the loss since it does not perceptibly affect his monetary worth. But losing the same amount of money on a bet may cause sadness if the loss has negative connotations regarding his judgment or luck.

Similarly, a psychiatrist criticized by a disturbed patient may not feel hurt if he thinks, "It doesn't mean anything." The same criticism by a colleague may substantially lower his self-esteem.

In terms of the model, sadness is produced when a person's evaluation of his domain is reduced. Whatever the actual stimulus situation, the individual (a) must perceive an event as a loss, and (b) the object or attribute that has been lost or downgraded must have some positive value. The loss of a wart would not cause sadness, whereas the loss of a finger would.

Differentiation from anger. The affective response

to downgrading by another person (insult, criticism) warrants further elaboration. If the criticism or insult is perceived as an unwarranted, unacceptable, or unjust intrusion, the individual becomes angry. If he accepts or believes the downgrading sufficiently to lower his evaluation of himself, then he feels sad. Similarly, if he considers that being made the recipient of the insult reflects badly on him, he is likely to feel sad.

Euphoria and Excitation

The essential condition for producing euphoria is a gain, i.e., increased evaluation of his domain by the individual. This may be produced by expansion of the boundaries of the domain, by the acquisition of new friends, development of new skills, or addition of new tangible objects, such as a new car. Or it may be produced by increased evaluation of the present components of the domain (such as a general elevation in the individual's self-evaluation). Examples are successful performance, leading to an increased evaluation of a particular ability; or an upgrading of the value of a material possession resulting from a compliment about it.

The meaning of a particular stimulus or object is a controlling factor in determining whether the individual experiences pleasure. For example, a person was shown a picture of a coat of arms; he was indifferent to it until it was pointed out that this might well be his family coat of arms. It then acquired a special meaning because it suggested that he might be of noble descent. Since the idea of noble lineage was a positive component of his value system, this led to a pleasant feeling.

Self-enhancement may have a substantial effect on motivation. Receiving a reward can result in generalized increase in expectancies of rewards, and consequently energize the individual to work more productively.

Feedback mechanisms may play a role in escalating the response to gains. It is possible that the subjective experience of euphoria after a self-enhancing event may be interpreted as further evidence that the event is a "good thing." (Cf. Valins, 1966, on effects of perception of inner states.) This interpretation may further enhance the value of the original stimulus.

Anxiety

The arousal of anxiety depends on the appraisal of a threat to the domain. Most frequently such threats are concerned with the danger of some physical or psychological injuries to the person. However, anxiety may be aroused by a threat to the safety, health, or well-being of any other person within the domain. Sometimes, the threat may be directed towards some institution with which the person is identified (for example, his community or his country) or towards a value, such as freedom.

Often the threat may consist of the danger of losing some object (inanimate or animate) that is important to the individual. For instance, a person may be afraid of losing his money or certain physical possessions. Or he may fear the loss of a friend or relative through geographical separation or through sickness or death of the other person.

Anxiety is enhanced by (a) appraisal that the individual cannot cope with or neutralize the threatening object; (b) immediacy of the perceived danger; (c) unpredictability of when the actual damage will occur; (d) high probability attached to the occurrence of the noxious event; (e) high degree of damage expected as a result of the noxious event.

Differentiation from sadness. When the loss has already occurred or when the domain has been devalued in expectation of a loss, sadness is produced. As long as the individual regards himself as still intact and the loss or other injury as only imminent, anxiety will occur.

Anger

Two conditions are essential for the production of anger. First, a particular stimulus is either immediately perceived as noxious or produces a strain on the individual by its impingement on his domain. The common types of noxious situations are: direct physical attack (or threat of attack) on the individual or his domain; or psychological attack (or threat) such as rejection, deprivation, criticism, insult, coercion. A strain or impingement on the domain may be defined as an interference with the functioning, expectations, goals, or comfort of the individual: thwarting, obstruction, distraction, intrusion.

Second, causality for the noxiousness or strain is attributed to the external object rather than o the individual himself. The putative cause of the strain has (in the judgment of the offended individual) violated some standard. For example, the violator has acted inappropriately or unreasonably.

This second condition is crucial in eliciting anger rather than anxiety or sadness.

In general terms, the noxious act is regarded as an *offense* and the perpetrator of the act as an *offender*. Typically, the focus is directed more to the offense and the offender than to the actual damage.

In customary interpersonal relations, the offense involves a violation or transgression (by somebody else) of the individual's code of acceptable behavior. This code consists of sets of rules ("shoulds" and "should nots") erected ostensibly to insure the smooth functioning of the individual and to protect him from psychological or physical damage. A strain on the domain is assessed in terms of whether it is appropriate, reasonable, justified. Anger is evoked if any of these standards is violated.

Differentiation from anxiety. For evocation of anxiety, the salient feature is danger: the individual is more concerned with the possibility of being damaged (or hurt) and with his perceived lack of coping devices to deal with the noxious stimulus. In the case of anger, the individual is more concerned with violation of rights and is less concerned with the possibility of danger to him.

Differentiation from sadness. When the main focus is on the actual loss in the domain (loss of self-esteem, loss of an object, etc.), sadness is produced. In anger-producing situations in contrast, the emphasis is on the violation of the individual's personal code. Even though the actual loss may be insignificant, a great deal of anger is proportional to the flagrancy of the wrong-doing; that is, by the degree of injustice, impropriety, inexcusability of the offense, and the degree of "badness" of the offender.

COGNITION IN PSYCHOPATHOLOGICAL DISORDERS

The ideational content leading to anxiety, sadness, euphoria, or anger is similar to the ideational content responsible for anxiety reactions, depression, mania, and paranoid states, respectively. The difference is that in psychopathology the ideational content represents a distortion of a realistic situation, whereas the normal cognitive responses encompass a reasonable approximation of the reality situation. The psychopathological condition, in other words, involves a thinking disorder.

A thinking disorder, in the absence of organic pathology, has generally been considered a pathognomic feature of schizophrenia (Kasanin, 1944; Lewis and Piotrowski, 1954). Depression, mania, and anxiety, in contrast, with their florid emotional manifestations, have been regarded, in essence, as affective disorders. Any cognitive abnormalities in depressions, mania, or anxiety reactions have been explained as the inevitable coloring of the ideation by the mood or, possibly, the result of the disorganizing properties of intense emotions.

A disorder in thinking, less gross and more specific than that described in schizophrenia, may be an important component of most of the common psychiatric syndromes. In a long term study of psychiatric patients, Beck (1963) observed that each of the patients systematically misconstrued certain types of experiences in an idiosyncratic way. These distortions of reality ranged from subtle inaccuracies in the mild neurotics to the familiar grotesque misinterpretations and delusions in the psychotics.

The distortions and misinterpretations are limited to the ideational content characteristic for each nosological group. Depressed patients, for example, tend to interpret their experiences in terms of their being deficient or deprived. Hence, a high proportion of their thought content includes ideas of being inferior, destitute, deserted, unloved, or physically deteriorated. Paranoid patients characteristically interpret neutral or innocuous cues as indications of abuse by some other person. Anxiety neurotics react to their experiences in terms of anticipation of personal danger, while hypomanic patients react with self-enhancing ideas.

The idiosyncratic ideation of the patients reveal systematic departures from reality and logic, including arbitrary inferences, selective abstractions, and overgeneralizations. This kind of paralogical thinking is found consistently only in the ideation with the idiosyncratic content. Other types of ideation do not appear to deviate from normal in this respect. Furthermore, the distorted ideas have several features in common. For example, they appear to arise automatically, without any apparent antecedent reflection or reasoning. They appear plausible to the patient even though implausible to other people. Finally, they are less amenable to change by reason or contradictory evidence than are other forms of ideation not associated with the specific form of psychopathology.

The typical feeling or emotional state of a patient appears to be a consequence of the way he structures reality. Hence, the depressed patient's feeling of sadness, loneliness, or guilt follows from his regarding himself as defective or blameworthy. Similarly, the anger of the paranoid is related to his ideas of being abused, and the apprehension of the anxiety neurotic stems from the perception of a threat. It is possible that there is a reciprocal interaction between the distorted ideas and the aroused feelings so that they tend to re-enforce each other.

There seems to be a continuum of cognitive impairment from the mild neurotic to severe psychotic. As the illness becomes intensified there is increasing impairment manifested by progressively greater degree of distortion, increasing perseveration of distorted ideas, and progressive impermeability of the distortions.

It is useful to characterize the specific diagnostic groups in terms of the specific content of the idiosyncratic ideation (Table 10.1).

The difference between anxiety, neurotic depression, and paranoia may be summarized as follows: the focus of the anxious patient is on the possibility of an attack; the paranoid patient focusses on the attack itself (the infringement on his boundaries); the depressed patient concentrates on a loss which he attributes to some inadequacy of his own. Apparently, the paranoid individual is concerned with injustice rather than actual loss; he reacts with anger rather than sadness.

IMPLICATIONS AND SPECULATIONS

The writer has delineated several distinct paradigms applicable to a broad range of human emotions: anxiety, anger, sadness, and elation. The stipulated antecedent conditions for instigating each of these affects can be readily tested with conventional experimental manipulations, such as the use of "stressor films." (Of course a film should be pre-tested to determine the meaning extracted by the subject instead of relying solely on the experimenter's a priori opinion.) If correct, this scheme provides a framework for evoking each of these affects in relatively pure culture. A presented stimulus intended to elicit anxiety, for instance, should be free of themes suggestive of injustice (which might evoke anger). A sequence of experiments, furthermore, can be designed to test the general proposition that a specific cognitive content determines the affective response.

The cognitive configurations outlined for the psychopathological disorders can also be used as the basis for experimental manipulations. Such an experiment with depressed patients (Loeb, Beck, and Diggory, 1970) indicated that immediate feedback of favorable information following performance of a task produced at least temporary improvement along several dimensions relevant to the depressed patients' self-devaluation.

The broader questions regarding the differences between normal and neurotic emotional responses cannot be adequately discussed within the scope of this chapter. Elsewhere, however, the writer has attempted to explain the neurotic patient's systematic bias in integrating and interpreting his experiences (Beck, 1963). According to this theory certain idiosyncratic cognitive schemas are overmobilized and disrupt the delicate matching of incoming data with appropriate cognitive categories. In anxiety reactions, for instance, conceptual systems relevant to danger override the more appropriate schemas and, consequently, stamp innocuous situations as dangerous.

Some systematic clinical studies support the postulation of such hyperactive schemas. When responsiveness to external stimuli is minimized, namely, during sleep, the imagery (dreams) of the depressed patient tends to center around the theme of loss: being deficient, losing in a competitive situation, or losing a valued object or person (Beck and Ward, 1961). Since these themes are also prominent in the patient's waking cognitions, it seems reasonable to postulate the activity of specific cognitive schemas in shaping the ideational content at various levels of consciousness. In other neurotic conditions, also, idiosyncratic schemas determine the way in which experiences are received, processed, interpreted, and stored.

Finally, a question may be raised regarding the origin of the idiosyncratic schemas and the life situations likely to activate them. The types of developmental experiences that stamp in unrealistic concepts relevant to the person and his world have been described previously (Beck, 1967). These schemas may remain latent for many years but, activated under certain stressful conditions, supersede more realistic concepts. The indiscriminate and repetitive application of these idiosyncratic schemas leads to a continual affective arousal. The "snowballing" phenomena observed in these conditions can be understood in terms of a feedback model. The affective responses to the cognitive distortions are in turn processed by the idiosyncratic cognitive systems and lead to further idiosyncratic cognitions. Thus, a continuous cycling of cognition-affect-cognition is established. The postulation of the feedback loop is supported, in part, by the finding by Schachter and Singer (1962) that the labelling of a state of arousal may be determined by the cognitive circumstances.

This model may be usefully applied to interrupting the exacerbation cycle of certain psychopathological conditions. Specific strategies, such as cognitive therapy (Beck, 1967), may be aimed at modifying the cognitive distortions; or interventions with drugs may be directed at damping down the intense affective state. The same model can also be adapted to understanding the cognitive dimension of certain social phenomena characterized by collective anger, anxiety, or apathy.

NOTE

1. The preparation of this chapter was supported by grants from the Marsh Foundation and Grant MH-16616 from the National Institute of Mental Health.

REFERENCES

American Psychiatric Association. 1968. *Diagnostic and Statistical Manual of Mental Disorders*. Washington: American Psychiatric Association.

Arnold, M.B. 1960. *Emotion and Personality*. New York: Columbia University Press.

Beck, A.T. 1963. Thinking and depression: 1. Idiosyncratic content and cognitive distortions. *Archives of General Psychiatry* 9:324-333.

----. 1967. *Depression: Clinical, Experimental, and Theoretical Aspects*. New York: Hoeber.

Beck, A.T., and Ward, C.H. 1961. Dreams of depressed patients: Characteristic themes in manifest content. *Archives of General Psychiatry* 5:462-467.

Bucknill, J. C., and Tuke, D. H. 1879. *A Manual of Psychological Medicine*. London: Churchill.

Gregory, I. 1968. *Fundamentals of Psychiatry*. Philadelphia: W.B. Saunders Company.

Kasanin, J.S. 1944. *Language and Thought in Schizophrenia*. Berkeley: University of California Press.

Kolb, L.C. 1968. *Noyes' Modern Clinical Psychiatry*. Philadelphia: W.B. Saunders Company.

Lazarus, R.S. 1966. *Psychological Stress and the Coping Process*. New York: McGraw Hill.

Lewis, N.D.C., and Piotrowski, Z.S. 1954. Clinical diagnosis of manic-depressive psychosis. *In* Hoch, P.H., and Zubin, J. (eds.), *Depression*. New York: Grune and Stratton, 25-38.

Loeb, A., Beck, A.T., and Diggory, J.C. 1971. Differential effects of success and failure on depressed and nondepressed patients. *Journal of Nervous and Mental Disease* 152:106-114.

Menninger, K. 1963. *The Vital Balance: The Life Process in Mental Health and Illness*. New York: Viking Press.

Schachter, S., and Singer, J.E. 1962. Cognitive, social

and physiological determinants of emotional state. *Psychological Review* 69:379-399.

Valins, S. 1966. Cognitive effects of false heart-rate feedback. *Journal of Personality and Social Psychology* 4:400-408.

11

Nicholas P. Spanos,
T. X. Barber and
Gerald Lang

Cognition and Self-Control: Cognitive Control of Painful Sensory Input

Eighty Ss were first tested for base-level response to a pain-producing stimulus and then were re-tested on the same pain stimulus after receiving 1 of 8 experimental treatments. The 8 treatments were arranged in a 2 x 2 x 2 factorial design: presence or absence of hypnotic-induction procedure; presence or absence of instructions for anesthesia; and presence or absence of demands for honest reports. Neither the hypnotic-induction procedure nor the demands for honesty affected the Ss' reports of the degree of pain experienced. The anesthesia instructions--"think of the hand as numb and insensitive as if it were a piece of rubber..."--produced an equal degree of pain reduction in hypnotic and non-hypnotic Ss and in Ss who were and those who were not exposed to demands for honesty. The results indicate that (a) Ss' reports of pain are less affected by demands for honesty and are more closely related to their actual experiences than has been previously assumed and (b) instructions which direct Ss to exercise cognitive control over painful sensory input are effective (with or without 'hypnosis') in reducing the experience of pain.

Overt and subjective responses to pain-producing

stimulation appear to be partially determined by cognitive factors. Beecher (1946) found that soldiers evacuated from battle areas complained very little about their severe wounds, reported very little pain, and often refused pain-relieving drugs, while civilians with equally severe wounds complained bitterly about their injuries, reported much pain, and almost always asked for pain-relieving medications. Beecher attributed the dramatic differences in the responses of the soldiers and civilians to the following cognitive factors: the soldiers defined their wounds as desirable events which gave them an honorable way to leave the battlefield, whereas the civilians interpreted their injuries as gross interferences with their everyday lives.

More recently, Nisbett and Schachter (1966) presented experimental data pointing to the importance of cognitive factors in determining pain experience. All subjects in the experiment were first given a "drug" (a placebo) and then were exposed to a pain stimulus (electric shock). Half of the subjects correctly believed that their tremors, palpitations, and other autonomic reactions were due to the electric shock, whereas the other half of the subjects were led to believe that their autonomic reactions were not due to the electric shock but, instead, were side effects of the "drug." Although all subjects received the same intensity of shock, those who believed that their autonomic reactions were due to the pain-producing stimulus reported that they experienced more pain than those who believed that their autonomic reactions were side effects of the "drug."

Similar findings were obtained in three subsequent studies. Bandler, Madaras, and Bem (1968) showed that subjects use their own overt behavioral responses to a constant aversive stimulus as evidence for deciding to what degree the stimulus was painful. Corah and Boffa (1970) replicated and extended the Bandler et al. findings and concluded that a cognitive factor--"a sense of control over the threatening stimulus"--plays an important role in determining the degree to which pain is experienced. Davison and Valins (1969) demonstrated that subjects perceive a noxious stimulus as less painful and are able to tolerate it longer when they are led to believe that they control the intensity of the stimulus.

The importance of cognitive factors was also illustrated by Zimbardo, Cohen, Weisenberg, Dworkin, and Firestone (1966). Reasoning from a cognitive dissonance framework, these investigators hypothesized that, with the intensity of the pain stimulus (electric shock) held constant, subjects (a) will experience reduced pain when they choose to undergo further pain with little external justification from the experimenter (high dissonance), but (b) will not experience reduced pain when they choose to undergo further pain only after much external justification has been provided (low dissonance). Both hypotheses were confirmed: the high cognitive dissonance group, but not the low dissonance group, showed a reduction in pain as indexed by verbal report, a behavioral response, and a physiological measure (GSR).

Studies demonstrating that responses to noxious stimuli are reduced by instructions or suggestions given under hypnosis also point to the effects of cognitive processes on pain. Since the experiment which we will present below is concerned with the effects on pain of instructions given with and without hypnosis, let us look more closely at the studies in this area.

A series of clinical reports (e.g., August, 1961; Bonilla, Quigley, and Bowers, 1961; Butler, 1954; Cangello, 1962; Esdaile, 1850; Perese, 1961) indicate that various types of pain (e.g., dental pain and the pain associated with childbirth, terminal carcinoma, and minor or major surgery) can be reduced by instructions or suggestions given to subjects who have been exposed to a hypnotic-induction procedure and who are judged to be in a state of hypnotic trance. However, as Barber (1959, 1963, 1969, 1970a, 1970b) has pointed out, very few clinical studies used control groups and reliable methods for assessing pain. Furthermore, the rare clinical studies that used control groups and unbiased methods of assessment invariably confounded the hypnotic-induction procedure (and the hypothetical hypnotic trance state) with instructions or suggestions intended to reduce pain, with the length and quality of the doctor-patient relationship, and with other important variables.

Although recent studies conducted in experimental laboratories employed standardized procedures for inducing pain and reliable methods of assessment, they did not always succeed in circumventing the methodological difficulties inherent in the clinical studies. In a series of experiments, Hilgard (1969) and Lenox (1970) found that suggestions of anesthesia were effective in reducing verbal and physiological indices of pain in subjects who had been exposed to a hypnotic -induction procedure and who were judged to be in hypnotic trance. Similar results were presented by Zimbardo, Rapaport, and Baron (1969), and by McGlashan, Evans, and Orne (1969). Although these experiments showed that combination of hypnotic-induction procedure with suggestions of anesthesia at times reduces pain, they did not demonstrate that hypnotic-induction procedures and the presumed hypnotic trance state were necessary or helpful in producing this effect. Each of these experiments confounded the hypnotic-induction procedure (and the presumed hypnotic state) with the suggestions of anesthesia. Although some of these experiments used a waking comparison group that was given a placebo or used waking subjects who were asked to act as if they were unresponsive to pain, none of the experiments used a waking control group that was given the same suggestions of anesthesia that were given to the hypnotic subjects. Consequently, it cannot be determined from these studies whether the reduction in reported pain was due to the hypnotic-induction procedure, to the presumed hypnotic trance state, to the suggestions of anesthesia, or to a combination of hypnotic induction or hypnosis with suggestions of anesthesia. Attempts to separate these variables were made in the experiments described next.

Barber and Hahn (1962) showed that waking subjects who are instructed to imagine pleasant situations show reductions in verbal and physiological indices of pain which equal the reductions exhibited by hypnotic subjects who are given suggestions of anesthesia. Subsequently, Barber and Calverley (1969) found that, as compared to a no-suggestion waking condition, a hypnotic-induction procedure (consisting primarily of repeated suggestions of relaxation, drowsiness, sleep, and deep hypnosis) was effective by itself in reducing reports of pain. However, these investigators also found that pain could be reduced to the same degree in subjects who had not been exposed to a hypnotic induction by (a) instruction to think of the stimulated limb as a piece of rubber that was numb and insensitive, and also by (b) instructions to concentrate on an interesting tape-recorded story during the application of the pain stimulus.

The above studies suggest that cognitive control of pain may be achieved in various ways: (a) leading the subject to believe that tremors, palpitations, and other autonomic responses produced by the pain stimulus are due to something else (e.g., a placebo-drug), (b) leading the subject to believe that he can control the intensity of the pain stimulus, (c) instructing the subject to think of the stimulated body part in a manner that is inconsistent with the perception of pain (e.g., to think of it as numb, insensitive, and made of rubber), or (d) instructing the subject to attend to events other than the pain-producing stimulation (e.g., to attend to an imagined pleasant scene or to an interesting tape-recorded narrative). These studies also indicate that, although hypnotic-induction procedures by themselves may at times reduce reports of pain, the experimental manipulations which are intended to produce cognitive control of pain (e.g., instructions to think of the limb as insensitive) are equally effective when they are given with or without a preceding hypnotic-induction procedure.

However, a major problem underlies most of the studies mentioned above. There is little doubt that at least some of the subjects were aware that they were participating in an experiment dealing with methods of reducing pain. These subjects may have reported a greater degree of reduction in pain than they actually experienced in order to comply with the demands of the experimental situation (Orne, 1962).

Bowers (1967) has cogently noted that more credible subjective reports may be obtained if subjects are questioned by a person other than the experimenter and are admonished to give honest reports. Although both hypnotic and non-hypnotic subjects who are exposed to such demands for honesty tend to report that suggested phenomena are less vivid and realistic than corresponding subjects who are not exposed to demands for honesty, the effects of demands for honesty on reports of pain have yet to be tested (Bowers, 1967; Spanos and Barber, 1968).

The aims of the present experiment[1] are (a) to assess the effectiveness of instructions aimed at engendering cognitive control over pain, (b) to evaluate the role of hypnotic-induction procedures on reports of pain, (c) to assess the credibility of subjects' pain reports by administering demands for honesty to half of the subjects, and (d) to assess the possible interactions among these variables.

METHOD

Subjects

Eighty male and female students (ages 17-25) attending two colleges in Massachusetts were asked to participate in an experiment on pain in which half of the subjects, selected at random, would be hypnotized and the others would not be hypnotized. None of the students had previously served as subjects in experiments conducted by the present authors. Sixty of the subjects were paid two dollars and the remaining twenty (all from a school having no contact with the 60 paid subjects) participated without being paid.

Base-Level (Pre-Treatment) Pain Test

Each subject was individually tested by one experimenter (WPS). Immediately after being seated, the subject was told that the experiment would begin, was asked to close his eyes, and the index finger of his right hand was placed in the Forgione-Barber pain stimulator (Forgione and Barber, 1971). Briefly, this apparatus consists of a sharp wedge which applies a 2000 gram weight to the finger for 60 seconds. After a minute, the experimenter removed the pain-producing stimulus, asked the subject to open his eyes, and left the room. His assistant (GL) then entered and presented the subject with a form to rate the degree of pain he had experienced on two 10-point Likert-type scales. The first scale was worded thus: Please circle the number that best represents your experience during the presentation of the weight on your finger. During the first 30 seconds, my finger felt:

0	1	2	3	4	5	6	7	8	9	10
Normal		Uncomfortable		Very Uncomfortable		Painful		Very Painful		Extremely Painful

The second scale was identical with the first with the exception that it asked the subject to rate what he had experienced during the second 30 seconds of stimulus presentation. Since it usually takes about 15 to 20 seconds for the Forgione-Barber pain apparatus to produce threshold pain, the subjects on the average rated the first 30 seconds of stimulus presentation as quite uncomfortable but not painful (mean rating was 3.2). The second 30 second rating of the stimulus presentation was used as the base-level response to the pain-producing stimulus.

Upon completing the base-level ratings, the assistant left the room and the experimenter re-entered and carried out the experimental treatments described next.

Experimental Treatments

Immediately upon completing the base-level test, each subject was randomly assigned, in order of his appearance for the experiment, to 1 of 8 treatment conditions which formed the cells of a 2 x 2 x 2 factorial experiment (hypnotic-induction versus no induction; anesthesia instructions versus no anesthesia instructions; and demands for honesty versus no demands for honesty). Ten subjects were assigned to each of the 8 cells of the factorial as illustrated in Table 11.1.

Hypnotic-induction procedure. As Table 11.1 shows, the 40 subjects assigned to groups 1-4 were exposed to a hypnotic-induction procedure. The induction procedure was standardized, lasted for 10 minutes, and was very similar to the one presented by Barber (1969, Appendix B). It included instructions designed to produce favorable attitudes and positive motivation toward hypnosis, repeated suggestions of eye-closure, relaxation, drowsiness, and sleep, and suggestions that the subject was entering a unique state (a hypnotic state) in which he would be able to experience those things that would be suggested.

Anesthesia instructions. Half of the subjects (groups 1, 2, 5, and 6) were given the following anesthesia instructions which were patterned after those employed by Barber and Calverley (1969):[2]

> I want you to succeed in not being disturbed by the weight by doing the following. Try to the best of your ability to imagine and think of your right hand as numb and insensitive. Think of your right hand as unable to sense any pain or discomfort. Please try to think of your hand as numb and insensitive as if it were a piece of rubber, until I take the weight off your finger. Other students were able to think of their hand in this way and it isn't as hard as it seems. What I want you to do is to control your thoughts and think continuously that your right hand has no feeling. Keep thinking that it is unable to feel any pain or discomfort. Continue to think of your hand as without pain, discomfort, or feeling of any kind. Please try to the very best of your ability to think continuously and to imagine vividly that your hand is numb, insensitive, and like a piece of rubber until the weight is off. Now keep thinking and vividly imagining that your right hand is becoming more and more numb and insensitive.

Upon completing one or both of the experimental treatments described above (hypnotic-induction procedure and/or anesthesia instructions), the experimenter administered the second (post-treatment) pain test to subjects in groups 1-6. The pain stimulus was applied to the middle finger of the subject's right hand for 60 seconds. (Subjects in groups 7 and 8 were told to close their eyes and were administered the second pain test without a preceding hypnotic-induction procedure or anesthesia instructions.)

After removing the pain stimulus, the experimenter

asked the subject to open his eyes and, if the subject was in one of the hypnotic groups, instructed him to awaken. The experimenter then left the room and the assistant entered.

Demands for honesty and post-treatment ratings of felt pain. The assistant asked the subject to rate again the intensity of his pain experience on the two Likert-type scales, one applying to the first 30 seconds of stimulus presentation and the other to the last 30 seconds. The ratings for the last 30 seconds of pain-stimulus presentation were used as the subjects' post-treatment ratings of pain.

Before making the post-treatment ratings, however, half of the subjects (groups 1, 3, 5 and 7) were given oral instructions by the assistant asking them to be honest when making their ratings. These demands for honesty, which were patterned after Bowers (1967), were worded as follows:

> I am going to give you a questionnaire about some of the experiences you just had with Mr. Spanos, but I would first like to stress the importance of your being as honest as you possibly can be when giving your answers. Let me elaborate a little and say that what what we really want you to do is to be honest with yourself in answering this questionnaire. The reason I am stressing this is that you might be tempted to think that saying you felt little or no pain is the correct answer for this experiment, and quite naturally you want to do well. But please do not mark the questionnaire in a certain way simply because you think it will please us. If, in fact, you felt little or no pain, that's fine, and of course we want you to say so. However, if you did feel a good deal of pain and discomfort, we want you to say that too. The only correct answer in this experiment, as far as you are concerned, is an honest one.

Self-Ratings of Hypnotic Depth

After completing their post-treatment pain ratings, each of the 40 subjects who had been assigned to the hypnotic groups (groups 1-4) was asked by the assistant to estimate his hypnotic depth. These ratings were made on a scale similar to the one constructed by Barber and Calverley (1966, pp. 423-424); it asked the subject to estimate the percentage of time during the administration of the second pain test that he was deeply, medium, lightly, or not hypnotized.

Upon completion of the experimental session each subject was admonished by the experimenter not to discuss the experiment with others until all subjects had been tested. Each subject stated that he understood the importance of this admonition and agreed to adhere to it.

RESULTS

Base-Level Pain Test

Prior to the experimental treatments, each subject was exposed to the pain-producing stimulation without receiving special instructions (base-level test). The subjects generally rated the last 30 seconds of this base-level test as painful--the mean rating was 5.8 with a rating of 6 indicating pain. During the last 30 seconds of the base-level test, 25% of the subjects rated their experience as very painful or extremely painful (ratings of 8 to 10), 34% rated it as painful (ratings of 6 or 7), 25% rated it as between very uncomfortable and painful (ratings of 4 or 5), and 16% rated it as uncomfortable (ratings of 2 or 3).

Effects of Experimental Treatments on Felt Pain

As Table 11.1 shows, Group 8 received the second pain test without being exposed to a hypnotic-induction procedure, to anesthesia instructions, or to demands for honesty. Subjects in Group 8 responded to the second pain test in the same way as the first test, that is, they rated their experience at about the level of pain (the mean rating was 5.7 during the second pain test and around 5.8 during the first pain test). These results indicate that, when not exposed to the experimental treatments, subjects experience the stimulus as borderline painful and the ratings of pain experience do not change when the stimulus is administered twice. Now let us turn to the results obtained on the second pain test with subjects who were exposed to one or more of the experimental treatments.

The ratings of felt pain were subjected to 2 x 2 x 2 analysis of covariance with the base-level ratings serving as the covariate and the post-treatment ratings as the dependent variable. The mean post-treatment pain ratings, adjusted by covariance for differences on the base-level test, are presented in Table 11.1.

The analysis of covariance showed that the anesthesia instructions significantly affected the pain ratings ($F = 5.24$, $df = 1/71$, $p < .05$). The mean pain rating was 4.5 for subjects receiving the anesthesia instructions (groups 1, 2, 5, and 6) and 5.8 for subjects not receiving the anesthesia instructions (groups 3, 4, 7, and 8). (A rating of 4 indicates very uncomfortable, and a rating of 6 indicates pain.) Of the subjects receiving the anesthesia instructions, 68% showed a reduction in reported pain below the base-level, whereas only 35% of the subjects who did not receive the anesthesia instructions showed a reduction. Only 17% of the subjects who received the anesthesia instructions showed increments in reported pain whereas 42% of the subjects who did not receive anesthesia instructions showed such increments.

The analysis of covariance did not show a significant main effect for the hypnotic-induction procedure; that is, the adjusted mean pain rating--5.0--of subjects who received the hypnotic induction (groups 1-4) did not differ significantly from the adjusted mean rating--5.3--of subjects who did not receive an induction (groups 5-8). Although there seemed to be a trend for subjects to report more pain when they were exposed to demands for honesty, the analysis of covariance showed that the adjusted mean pain rating--5.4--of subjects who were exposed to demands for honesty (groups 1, 3, 5, and 7) did not differ significantly from the mean rating--4.9--of subjects who were not exposed to demands for honesty (groups 2,4,6, and 8). Also, the analysis of covariance showed that the three independent variables (hypnotic induction, anesthesia instructions, and demands for honesty) did not yield significant two-way or three-way interactions.

In brief, the anesthesia instructions were effective in reducing reports of pain; combining the anesthesia

TABLE 11.1. Adjusted Mean Pain Ratings

	Hypnotic Induction		*No Hypnotic Induction*		*Total Mean*
	Anesthesia Instructions	*No Anesthesia Instructions*	*Anesthesia Instructions*	*No Anesthesia Instructions*	
Demands for Honesty	4.4 (Group 1)	5.6 (Group 3)	4.9 (Group 5)	6.8 (Group 7)	5.4
No Demands for Honesty	4.7 (Group 2)	5.3 (Group 4)	3.9 (Group 6)	5.7 (Group 8)	4.9
Total Mean	4.6	5.4	4.4	6.2	5.2

Note: Mean for *hypnotic induction* (groups 1-4) is 5.0. Mean for *no hypnotic induction* (groups 5-8) is 5.3. Mean for *anesthesia instructions* (groups 1, 2, 5, and 6) is 4.5. Mean for *no anesthesia instructions* (groups 3, 4, 7, and 8) is 5.8.

instructions with the hypnotic-induction procedure did not produce a greater reduction in pain than giving the anesthesia instructions alone; subjects who were and those who were not exposed to demands for honesty did not report significantly different degrees of pain; and there were no significant interactions between anesthesia instructions, hypnotic-induction procedure, and demands for honesty.

Self-Ratings of Hypnotic Depth

Post-experimentally, the 40 subjects who had been exposed to the hypnotic-induction procedure were asked to rate the degree to which they felt they were hypnotized during the second (post-treatment) pain stimulation. Twenty-three per cent rated their hypnotic depth as medium or deep, 62% rated it as light, and 15% rated themselves as not hypnotized. A Pearson correlation coefficient was computed between the subjects' ratings of their hypnotic depth and their ratings of the degree of pain reduction, that is, the degree to which they rated the stimulus as less painful during the second (post-treatment) pain test as compared to the first (base-level) pain test. Although there was a tendency for those who reported greater hypnotic depth to also report a greater degree of pain reduction, the correlation (r = .22) was not statistically significant.

DISCUSSION

A substantial body of data (Andersen and Sarbin, 1964; Barber, 1969, 1970a, 1970b; Barber and Calverley, 1962, 1966) indicates that test-suggestions for arm rigidity, hand levitation, amnesia, etc., generally give rise to very similar overt responses and subjective experiences in (a) subjects who have been exposed to suggestions of relaxation, drowsiness, sleep, and deep hypnosis (hypnotic subjects), and in (b) subjects who have been simply exhorted to try to experience those things that are suggested (task-motivated controls). Furthermore, the subjective reports of hypnotic subjects appear to be closely related to the wording of the test-suggestions (Spanos, 1971; Spanos and Barber, 1972). For instance, hypnotic subjects who are given suggestions to imagine a rising balloon tied to their arm tend to experience arm levitation as non-volitional ("it rose by itself"), whereas hypnotic subjects who are given direct suggestions that their arm is rising tend to experience arm levitation as volitional ("I made it rise"). These findings suggest that the overt behaviors and subjective experiences of both hypnotic subjects and controls may be conceptualized more parsimoniously as resulting from cognitive processes that are engendered by the wording of the test-suggestions rather than by positing the existence of a unique 'state of trance' operating in the hypnotic subjects but not in the controls.

The results of the present experiment, and also the results of previous experiments (Barber and Calverley, 1969; Barber and Hahn, 1962) are congruent with this interpretation, indicating that instructions designed to produce cognitive control over pain give rise to a reduction in reported pain in subjects who have not been exposed to a hypnotic-induction procedure. The anesthesia instructions used in this experiment and also in the experiment by Barber and Calverley (1969) told the subject to do two things. First, the instructions informed the subject that he could control his sensory experiences and that such control had been successfully exercised by previous subjects. Second, the instructions provided the subject with a cognitive strategy for exercising control over pain. The instruction asked the subject to create in his imagination a situation which is inconsistent with the experience of pain, that is, the subject was asked to imagine and think of his hand, not as a limb capable of feeling pain, but as one which is numb and insensitive. These instructions were effective in reducing pain in both hypnotic subjects and controls.

The admonitions of honesty did not significantly affect the subjects' reports of pain. This outcome suggests that (a) subjects' reports of pain are less affected by demands for honesty and are more closely related to their subjective experiences than we had previously assumed, and (b) the anesthesia instructions affected the subjects' pain experience and not only their verbal reports of pain. The hypothesis that anesthesia instructions modify subjects' experience receives further support from the studies of Barber and Calverley (1969),

Barber and Hahn (1962), Hilgard (1969), Lenox (1970), and Zimbardo, Rapaport, and Baron (1969). These investigators found that physiological indices of pain, which are not under direct voluntary control, are reduced along with verbal reports of pain when suggestions or instructions for anesthesia are administered.

In the present experiment, the hypnotic-induction procedure per se did not significantly affect reports of pain. Also, subjects who rated themselves as more deeply hypnotized did not show a significantly greater reduction in pain than those who rated themselves as less deeply hypnotized. These results are in line with most previous studies in this area, reviewed by Barber (1970b) and Hilgard (1969), which generally found that a hypnotic-induction procedure per se (without instructions for anesthesia) did not significantly reduce reported pain. The results also support the earlier findings of Barber and Calverley (1969) that procedures designed to enhance cognitive control over painful sensory input are effective in reducing pain when they are given without a hypnotic-induction procedure. In more general terms, the results are consistent with a growing body of literature which indicates that cognitive factors play an important role in determining the effects of sensory input, and that procedures which direct subjects to think of the stimulated body part in a manner which is inconsistent with the perception of pain are effective means of reducing discomfort and pain.

NOTES

1. This research was supported in part by grants (MH-11521 and MH-19152) to T.X. Barber from the National Institute of Mental Health, U.S. Public Health Service. We are indebted to John McPeake of Massasoit Junior College and Bernard Phillips of Boston University for assistance in obtaining subjects.

2. Groups 1 and 2 received the anesthesia instructions immediately upon completion of the hypnotic-induction procedure and without a break in the continuity of presentation. Groups 5 and 6 received the anesthesia instructions without a preceding hypnotic-induction procedure.

REFERENCES

Andersen, M.L., and Sarbin, T.R. 1964. Base rate expectancies and motoric alterations in hypnosis. *International Journal of Clinical and Experimental Hypnosis* 12:147-158.

August, R.V. 1961. *Hypnosis in Obstetrics*. New York: McGraw-Hill.

Bandler, R.J., Jr., Madaras, G.R., and Bem, D.J. 1968. Self-observation as a source of pain perception. *Journal of Personality and Social Psychology* 9:205-209.

Barber, T.X. 1959. Toward a theory of pain: Relief of chronic pain by prefrontal leucotomy, opiates, placebos, and hypnosis. *Psychological Bulletin* 56:430-460.

----. 1963. The effects of "hypnosis" on pain: A critical review of experimental and clinical findings. *Psychosomatic Medicine* 25:303-333.

----. 1969. *Hypnosis: A Scientific Approach*. New York: Van Nostrand Reinhold.

----. 1970a. *LSD, Marihuana, Yoga, and Hypnosis*. Chicago: Aldine.

----. 1970b. Suggested ("hypnotic") behavior: The trance paradigm versus an alternative paradigm. Harding, Mass.: Medfield Foundation.

Barber, T.X., and Calverley, D.S. 1962. "Hypnotic" behavior as a function of task motivation. *Journal of Psychology* 54:363-389.

----. 1966. Toward a theory of hypnotic behavior: Experimental evaluation of Hull's postulate that hypnotic susceptibility is a habit phenomenon. *Journal of Personality* 34:416-433.

----. 1968. Toward a theory of "hypnotic" behavior: Replication and extension of experiments by Barber and co-workers (1962-65) and Hilgard and Tart (1966). *International Journal of Clinical and Experimental Hypnosis* 16:179-195.

----. 1969. Effects of hypnotic induction, suggestions of anesthesia, and distraction on subjective and physiological responses to pain. Paper presented at Eastern Psychological Association Annual Meeting, Philadelphia, April 10.

Barber, T.X., and Hahn, K.W., Jr. 1962. Physiological and subjective responses to pain-producing stimulation under hypnotically-suggested and waking-imagined "analgesia". *Journal of Abnormal and Social Psychology* 55:411-418.

Beecher, H.K. 1946. Pain in men wounded in battle. *Annals of Surgery* 123:98-105.

Bonilla, K.B., Quigley, W.F., and Bowers, W.F. 1961. Experience with hypnosis on a surgical service. *Military Medicine* 126:364-366.

Bowers, K.S. 1967. The effects of demands for honesty on reports of visual and auditory hallucinations. *International Journal of Clinical and Experimental Hypnosis* 15:31-36.

Butler, B. 1954. The use of hypnosis in the care of the cancer patient. *Cancer* 7:1-14.

Cangello, V.W. 1962. Hypnosis for the patient with cancer. *American Journal of Clinical Hypnosis* 4:215-226.

Corah, N.L., and Boffa, J. 1970. Perceived control, self-observation, and response to aversive stimulation. *Journal of Personality and Social Psychology* 16:1-4.

Davison, G.C., and Valins, S. 1969. Maintenance of self-attributed and drug-attributed behavior change. *Journal of Personality and Social Psychology* 11:25-33.

Esdaile, J. 1850. *Mesmerism in India*. Republished in 1957 as *Hypnosis in Medicine and Surgery*. New York: Julian Press.

Forgione, A., and Barber, T.X. 1971. A strain gauge pain stimulator. *Psychophysiology* 8:102-106.

Hilgard, E.R. 1969. Pain as a puzzle for psychology and physiology. *American Psychologist* 24:103-113.

Lenox, J.R. 1970. Effects of hypnotic analgesia on verbal report and cardiovascular response to ischemic pain. *Journal of Abnormal Psychology* 75:199-206.

McGlashan, T.H., Evans, F.J., and Orne, M.T. 1969. The nature of hypnotic analgesia and placebo response to experimental pain. *Psychosomatic Medicine* 31:227-246.

Nisbett, R.E., and Schachter, S. 1966. Cognitive manipulation of pain. *Journal of Experimental Social Psychology* 2:227-236.

Orne, M.T. 1962. On the social psychology of the

psychological experiment: with particular reference to demand characteristics and their implications. *American Psychologist* 17:776-783.

Perese, D.M. 1961. How to manage pain in malignant disease. *Journal of the American Medical Association* 175:75-81.

Spanos, N.P. 1971. Goal-directed fantasy and the performance of hypnotic test suggestions. *Psychiatry* 34:86-96.

Spanos, N.P., and Barber, T.X. 1968. "Hypnotic" experiences as inferred from subjective reports: Auditory and visual hallucinations. *Journal of Experimental Research in Personality* 3:136-150.

----. 1972. Cognitive activity during "hypnotic" suggestibility: Goal-directed fantasy and the experience of non-volition. *Journal of Personality* 40: 510-524.

Zimbardo, P.G., Cohen, A.R., Weisenberg, M., Dworkin, L., and Firestone, I. 1966. Control of pain motivation by cognitive dissonance. *Science* 151:217-219.

Zimbardo, P.G., Rapaport, C., and Baron, J. 1969. Pain control by hypnotic induction of motivational states. *In* P. Zimbardo (ed.), *The Cognitive Control of Motivation*. Chicago: Scott, Foresman.

12

George O. Klemp and
Howard Leventhal

Self-Persuasion and Fear Reduction from Escape Behavior

A study was run to replicate and extend an experiment by Bandler, Madaras, and Bem (BMB). The BMB study demonstrated that subjects rated an electrical shock as more uncomfortable when they chose to escape the shock than when (a) they chose to sustain their exposure, or when (b) their exposure to the shock was controlled by the experimenter. The subjects' escape behavior functioned as a communication: It persuaded him that the shock he chose to escape was more uncomfortable. The central hypothesis in the present study was that the self-persuasion effect occurs only when the subject has a high degree of tolerance for shock. Thus, a subject's own behavior was expected to be salient to him if he had high shock tolerance but less salient to him if he had a low tolerance for shock. The hypothesis was supported by the results. The results also showed that shock duration is an important methodological factor; longer shocks are more painful than shorter ones.

Daryl Bem (1965, 1966, 1967) suggests that to some extent individuals infer their beliefs from their own behavior. Behavior is overt and open to social definition and provides, therefore, more precise information than the internal cues produced by attitudes and beliefs. To make his point, Bem suggests that when a person formulates his attitudes he behaves just like an external observer; that is, he attributes beliefs to himself to explain his observed behavior (Kelley, 1967).

Critics of Bem's position have suggested that the processes of evaluating stimuli, attitude formation, and change are different in the observer and actor. Observers are said to infer beliefs from behavior because they lack information on the actor's private attitudes. Actors, however, already have beliefs and are not expected to change them unless they have no way of justifying a discrepancy between their overt actions and their private attitudes. (Jones, Linder, Kiesler, Zanna, and Brehm, 1968; Piliavin, Piliavin, Lowenton, McCauley, and Hammond, 1969).

To counter the above criticism, Bem has attempted to demonstrate that inference, or self-persuasion from behavior, occurs in actors. In one such demonstration, Bandler, Madaras, and Bem (1968) found that *S*s changed judgments about the discomfort of a standard electric shock if they chose to escape it. Each subject received a series of shocks. A half second after shock onset, one of three signals appeared: an Escape, a Sustain, or a Reaction Time (RT) signal. In the Escape signal condition the subject was instructed: "You should press the button and turn off the shock unless the shock is not uncomfortable in which case you may elect not to depress the buttom. The choice is up to you." In the Sustain signal condition the subject was instructed: "You should not press the button and turn off the shock. However, if the shock is so uncomfortable that you feel you must turn it off, you may. Again, the choice is up to you." The shock lasted for two full seconds. For the RT signal condition the subject was told that the "... time that it takes you to press the button..." will be recorded and the "depression of the button may or may not turn off the shock." Each subject experienced all conditions in random order. When the average rating of shock was calculated it was found that the standard shock was rated as more painful on the Escape trials than on either the Sustain or RT trials. There were no differences in the ratings of the RT and the Sustained shocks. The Bandler, Madaras and Bem study (BMB) strongly suggests that the actor's behavior is self-persuading;

it helps him to form his belief about the shock. The subject's escape behavior implies that the stimulus is severe--leading him to believe that the shock was uncomfortable.

Although it appears that an actor can behave like an observer there are reasons to assume that this process is atypical for subjects in stress settings. The typical subject has at least two important sources of information in addition to his escape behavior: 1. external cues generated by the painful shock, and 2. internal cues generated by his fear and distress (Leventhal, 1970). When *S* escapes a shock, he might experience reductions of pain, fear, and distress, and as a consequence he may judge the escaped shock as less uncomfortable. Indeed, several studies demonstrate that when subjects control the termination of a stress stimulus they are less disturbed by it than are *S*s who have no control over a set of identical shocks (Mowrer and Vieck, 1948; Pervin, 1963; Weiss, 1968). The BMB study suggests, albeit indirectly, that choice and the connection of escape with discomfort can lead subjects to ignore their private information (pain and distress) and to behave like observers.

The study reported in this chapter[1] is a replication and extension of the BMB study. The goal of the extension was to locate stimulus and subject parameters which might influence the relative strength of these two processes: self-persuasion from behavior or judgments based upon changing stimulus attributes. Since the original procedures, particularly the Escape and Sustain instructions, were followed as closely as possible, a replication of the BMB results was anticipated--if the subject chooses to escape shock he will evaluate it as more uncomfortable than if he chooses to sustain his exposure to it.

The extension varied two factors not manipulated in the BMB study: 1) the duration of exposure to shock before the appearance of the action signal, and 2) the subject's apprehensiveness of or tolerance for painful stimulation. Both long exposure to shock and high sensitivity to shock were expected to increase the amount of attention the subject gave to the stimulus and the distress caused by it and to reduce the self-persuasion effect from behavior.

In the BMB study the shock was on for 1/2 second when the Escape, Sustain, or RT signals appeared. Thus, in all conditions the subject had at least 1/2 second to evaluate the stimulus before attending to his response task. In the present study the time available to the *S* for appraising the stimulus was varied by using three different durations of shock prior to the signal: a) a zero-second shock, the shock and signal appearing simultaneously, b) a 1/2 second shock, the signal appearing 1/2 second after the shock began, and c) a one-second shock, the signal appearing one second after the shock began. It was predicted that longer shocks, probably because they can be appraised more accurately, will lead *S*s to base judgments of discomfort more on intensity of shock than upon behavior. Moreover, when the signal is set to appear at shock onset there will be a greater difference in duration between escaped and sustained shocks, and this should favor judgment of increased comfort following escaped shock.

Prior to the experimental trials each subject evaluated the discomfort of a series of shocks. One of these shocks, a shock rated near the top of the discomfort scale, was used for the experimental trials. The procedure was used to achieve subjective rather than physical equivalence of the standard shock and also allowed an assessment of *S*s' shock tolerance. Subjects who took little shock before reaching the top of the rating scale were relatively fearful and avoidant and were characterized as low tolerance subjects. Subjects who took a great deal of shock before reaching the upper boundary of the scale were relatively calm and relaxed and were characterized as high tolerance *S*s. Since low tolerance *S*s are fearful, they are likely to be more responsive to the shock per se than to the implications of escape behavior. The unfearful, high tolerance subject is the opposite; his instrumental (escape) behavior is more salient to him than the pain and fear of shock. The information salient to the high tolerance subject is similar, therefore, to that of the observer and he will show the self-persuasion effect. The low tolerance *S* will not.

METHOD

Design and Subjects

Sixty-three male undergraduates were recruited through the introductory psychology subject pool. They did not know when they volunteered that the study used electric shock, but they were informed of this when they appeared for the experiment, and were given the option of leaving without losing credit for participation. Only two of 63 students refused. The data of seven additional *S*s were deleted because each failed to follow instructions (they escaped on one or more Sustain trials or stayed on three or more Escape trials).

The within-subject design was the same as that in the BMB study. Every subject served in each of three experimental conditions: Escape, Sustain, and RT, and the effect of escape was tested by within-subject comparisons. The between-subject factors were: 1) three durations (0, 1/2, 1 second) of exposure to shock before the appearance of the signal with 18 *S*s in each duration, and 2) tolerance for shock; the entire sample was divided into three levels of shock tolerance, high, middle, and low.

Procedure

The *S* was seated at a table which held the three main pieces of apparatus: a signal box with three colored lights, a momentary action pendant switch for responding, and a hand rest for the right hand. The tips of the third and fourth fingers of the right hand were treated with a silver chloride electrode paste to which silver disk electrodes of the Lykken type (1959) were attached. The shock was delivered by an electronic stimulator which produced a 60 cycle/second constant current. The intensity of the output varied from 0.10 to 5.50 mA ± 2%, in 48 equal appearing steps (Stevens, Carter, and Shickman, 1958).

A graphic representation of a 7-point semantic

differential scale, ranging from "1" (not comfortable) to "7" (very uncomfortable), was also on the table. Each subject used the scale to rate a series of .5 second shocks which were gradually increased in strength. In this way an individual continuum of discomfort was established. For each *S* the experimenter recorded the strongest shock to which the subject gave a "1" rating and the strongest shock to which he gave a "6" rating. The distribution of shock intensities of all *S*s for the six ratings was used to divide the *S*s into low, moderate, and high tolerance groups.

Duration of Shock before Appearance of the Signal. After rating the series of .5 second shocks the *S* was told that on each of the following trials a shock would be paired with a panel light. A third of the *S*s were told that the shock and light would appear simultaneously, another third that the light would appear 1/2 second after shock onset, and the remaining third that the light would appear one second after shock onset. This instruction and the actual stimulus presentation established the 3 durations.

Mode of Response. Following the instructions outlined above, the subject was given the momentary action pendant switch and was told that it ould be used to terminate the shocks. Using the instructions of the BMB study (1968:206), the experimenter explained that three different lights would be used to signal the response conditions:

1. *Escape Condition:* "This is the red condition (illuminated red light). In the red condition you will be able to turn off the shock by pressing the button in your left hand. In this condition, the red condition, you *should* press the button and turn off the shock. However, if the shock is not uncomfortable you may elect not to depress the button. The choice is up to you."

2. *Sustain Condition:* "This is the green condition (illuminated green light). In the green condition the button in your left hand will enable you to turn off the shock. In this condition, the green condition, you

should not press the button and turn off the shock. However, if the shock is so uncomfortable that you feel you must turn it off, you may. Again the choice is up to you."

3. *RT Condition:* "This is the yellow condition (illuminated yellow light). The yellow condition is a reaction time condition. We are interested in recording the time it takes you to press the button once the yellow light comes on. Therefore, please press the button as soon as the yellow light is illuminated. *Your* depression of the button *may* or *may not* turn off the shock." On five of the ten RT trials depressing the pendant switch terminated the shock; on the remaining five the shock lasted for a full two seconds as did all unterminated shocks. Thus, the mean discomfort ratings could be computed separately for the RT shocks which terminated and which continued. This permitted us to compare those shocks terminated by choice (Escape condition) and those terminated by chance (RT Terminate condition), and to compare shocks that are continued by choice (Sustain condition) and continued by chance (RT Continue condition). Such comparisons control for duration.

The subjects were told that unterminated shocks would last two seconds, and they were instructed to rate each shock on the 7-point scale immediately following the trial. The instructions were repeated in an abbreviated form, choice was emphasized, and the subject was asked if he had any questions.

Unknown to the subject the shock stimulus was set at the level he had previously rated as "6" on 30 of the 34 experimental trials. These 30 trials were divided equally among the three signal conditions. The 4 remaining shocks were set at Level 1 to give the impression that the experimenter was varying intensity over a wide range. Responses to the "1" shocks were excluded from the analyses. The response conditions were randomized for each subject, as was the order of trials. The scores for each subject consisted of the average shock ratings for each of the three response conditions. Reaction times were recorded in the Escape and RT conditions on a Standard Electric model S-1 reaction timer.

RESULTS

The first question is whether choosing to escape increases the rated discomfort of the shock stimulus. There is a highly significant difference between the means for Escape, Sustain, and RT conditions ($F = 12.50$, $df = 2/90$, $p < .001$). But the direction of the effect is opposite to that predicted from the self-persuasion hypothesis. Thus, shocks in the Escape condition ($\bar{X} = 4.89$) are rated as significantly less uncomfortable than shocks in the Sustain conditions ($\bar{X} = 5.22$).

Shock Duration and Discomfort

Why is the Escaped shock rated as less uncomfortable than the Sustained or the RT shock? The simplest possibility is that the escaped shock is less painful because it is of shorter duration. Evidence for a duration effect is seen in a significant interaction ($F = 7.08$, $df = 4/90$, $p < .001$) between duration and mode of response. When the shock lasts for a full second before the appearance of the reaction signals there are relatively small differences between conditions in the actual duration of shock (mean shock duration of 1.61 seconds in Escape compared to 2 seconds in Sustain) and small differences in the rated discomfort of shock (Figure 12.1). By contrast, when there is a zero-second delay between shock onset and response signal the actual difference in shock duration is maximal (mean shock duration of .83 seconds for Escape versus 2.00 seconds for Sustain) and the difference in discomfort rating is also at its maximum. These comparisons ignore tolerance levels.

Tolerance and Self-Persuasion

The finding of greatest theoretical importance is that of a significant interaction between the variables of tolerance level and mode of response ($F = 5.00$; $df = 4/90$; $p < .005$). The mean ratings for shock discomfort are presented in Table 12.1. The RT Terminated and RT Continued shocks were analyzed as separate conditions and are presented that way in the table. The interaction can best be understood by examining the

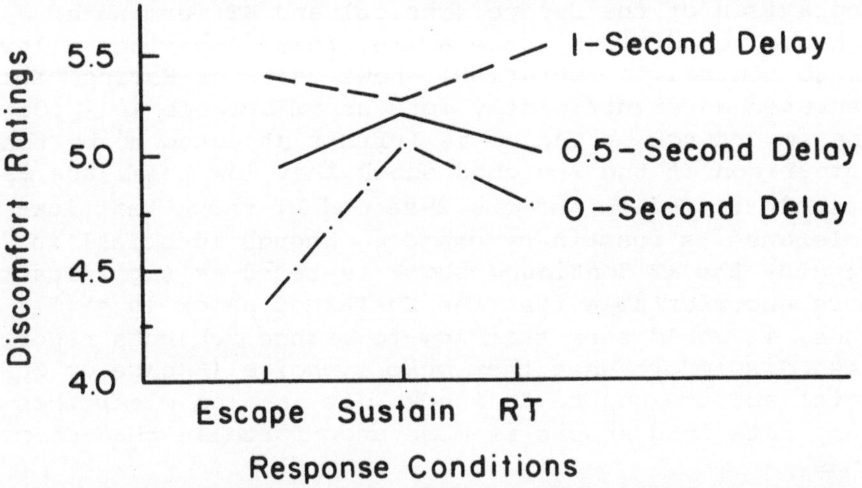

FIGURE 12.1. The effects of shock duration and response mode upon discomfort ratings.

differences between response modes for each level (high, moderate, low) of shock tolerance. The probability values reported for comparisons between specific pairs of means were calculated by the conservative Tukey A Comparisons Test (Winer, 1962).

High tolerance subjects are expected to show the self-persuasion effect; they are relatively unafraid and insensitive to shock. Their escape behavior is likely to be salient to them. As expected, then, they rate the Escaped shock as significantly more uncomfortable than the RT Terminated shock ($p < .01$); that is controlling for shock duration, the shock they escaped by choice is rated as more uncomfortable than the shock terminated by chance. Choosing to sustain shock has no effect upon discomfort; the Sustained shock is rated (5.32) virtually the same as the RT Continued shock (5.27). Both of the longer shocks (Sustained and RT Continued) are judged more uncomfortable than both of the briefer shocks (Escaped and RT Terminated).

The low tolerance subjects are relatively fearful and

sensitive to the pain of shock. Thus, when the shock is escaped by choice one expects them to feel less discomfort than when the shock is terminated by chance. A comparison of the Escape (choice) and RT Terminated (chance) conditions (once again, this comparison allows us to control for duration) shows that the Escaped shock is rated as significantly less uncomfortable ($p < .01$). The importance of choice is further attested to by the comparison of the 2-second shock that low tolerance *S*s sustain by choice and the 2-second RT shock that low-tolerance *S*s sustain by chance. Though identical in length, the RT Continued shock is rated as significantly more uncomfortable that the Sustained shock ($p < .01$). Thus, it would seem that low-tolerance subjects report less discomfort when they make a choice (Escape or Sustain) about exposure to shock. It is also clear that they rate long shocks as more uncomfortable than short ones.

TABLE 12.1. Effects of Shock Tolerance and Response Mode Upon Shock Discomfort.

Initial Tolerance Level	*Response Mode* *Escape*	*Sustain*	*Reaction Time* *Terminate*	*Continue*
High*	4.94_a	5.32_b	4.41_c	5.27_b
Moderate	4.88_a	5.18_b	5.03_{ab}	5.23_b
Low	4.86_a	5.14_b	5.24_b	5.56_c
Overall Mean	4.89	5.22	4.89	5.35

* Within each row of the table those means with different subscripts are significantly different from one another at better than the $p < .05$ level. All comparisons are by the Tukey A test (Winer, 1962).

Results for the middle tolerance group are between the results for high- and low-tolerance subjects. The significantly different cells are shown in Table 12.1. The middle tolerance *S*s show no clear effect. Their ratings of the brief shocks (Escape and RT Terminated) are not significantly different and the same is true for their ratings of the longer shocks (Sustained and RT Continued).

DISCUSSION

The findings of the present study extend those of the BMB study. First, the self-persuasion effect did not appear for the entire sample; escaping from shock increased discomfort ratings only for the high-tolerance subjects. Second, brief shocks were found less uncomfortable than longer shocks. Both findings differ from those reported in the BMB study.

Some of the noncomparability of results between the studies could be due to differences in the electric shock apparatus. The shock generator in the present study produced a constant current, square-wave AC shock. In the BMB study a DC inductorium was used and its current output was apparently quite variable.[2] It is possible that the change from DC to AC or the change from an uneven stimulus output to a square-wave output is responsible for the differences in results. There is some evidence that AC and DC shocks are perceived differently; the AC shocks become much more uncomfortable with longer durations of exposure (Leventhal, Brown, and Klemp, Mimeo). This difference may account for the strong duration effects reported in the present experiment, but it is less clear how it would affect the self-persuasion phenomenon. It is possible that AC shocks minimize self-persuasion because they keep *S*s at a higher fear level. This could happen if there was less adaptation to an AC stimulus. If a subject adapts to a DC shock he will become less fearful of it and thus facilitate self-persuasion. Two signs indicate that there is less adaptation to AC than to DC shocks: (1) longer AC shocks are substantially more painful than shorter ones, and (2) over the experimental trials of the present study there was relatively little decrease in discomfort reported of the shock rated "6". The decrease in discomfort was much greater for the DC shock used in the BMB study.

It also seems likely that subjects in the present study were far more shock sensitive than those used by Bandler, Madaras, and Bem. If this were true, it would help explain the decrease in the self-persuasion effect.

Our subjects were drawn from an introductory Psychology pool and were unaware before the experimental session that they would be exposed to electric shock. In contrast, the subjects in the BMB study were engineering students, probably had more experience with shock, and judging from the BMB method section, they knowingly volunteered for a study on electric shock. If we assume that BMB sampled high-tolerance subjects and that their DC shock apparatus produced equally painful shocks at long and short durations, we can probably reconcile most of the differences between the studies.

What, then, can we conclude about the self-persuasion effect? It is still our judgment that Bandler, Madaras, and Bem reported a real effect. However, it appears that an important characteristic of the subject, in particular, his tolerance for shock, is a limiting variable. Self-persuasion from one's instrumental escape behavior occurs only for high-shock-tolerance subjects. Low-tolerance subjects show an opposite pattern--after choosing to escape a shock they rate it as less uncomfortable than a shock which is escaped without choice.

We cannot, however, clearly define the mechanism that mediates the change in judgmental process as we move from high- to low-tolerance subjects, though we can enumerate some of the possibilities. First, it is conceivable that the change in judgment, from increased to decreased discomfort with escape, is cognitively mediated, that is, it may reflect a difference in cognitive set with low tolerance *S*s oriented toward getting away from or minimizing the painful stimulus. From this perspective, successful control of duration would be rewarding and produce judgments of reduced discomfort, despite the implication of the experimental instructions that one has chosen to escape the more painful shocks.

A second possibility is that differences in emotional arousal are necessary for the change in judgment. Low tolerance *S*s may be more frightened, that is, they show more of the bodily components of fear, and fear might intensify the judged discomfort of shock. If being able to choose is critical in reducing this fear, we would expect lower discomfort ratings in the choice conditions, Escape and Sustain, than in the RT conditions, Terminated and Continued. A third possibility is that the low-tolerance subjects felt compelled, that is, had no choice, to escape the painful shock, and this eliminated the self-persuasion effect.

Our data suggest that the third possibility, the elimination of choice, was not the mediator of these effects. While we have no verbal measure of choice, the actual response times show that 80% of the subjects, regardless of their tolerance for shock, took more time to respond in Escape than RT conditions. It seems reasonable to conclude, therefore, that when subjects were confronted by the Escape signal they were making a decision about responding.

Because the major difference between high- and low-tolerance subjects appears with the absence of choice--low tolerance *S*s rated the RT Terminated shock as very uncomfortable--the data tend to support the emotional mediation hypothesis. But the cognitive set, the orientation to getting away from the shock, may be a consequence of the emotional arousal. Thus, studies are needed which independently manipulate emotional state and cognitive orientation. At present, we can only conclude that sensitivity to shock is an important modifier of the self-persuasion effect. Low-tolerance subjects, because of their cognitive set to control the duration of the stimulus or because of their bodily arousal state, do not respond to the BMB instructions by adopting an observer's attitude in explaining the consequences of their escape behavior. Their behavior and its implications are less salient to them than other internally relevant sources of information.

NOTES

1. The data reported were drawn from the M.A. thesis of the first-listed author. The research was supported by Grants Numbers HS 00436 and NU 00302 from the U.S. Public Health Service.

2. Daryl Bem suggested this possibility in a discussion of the experimental outcomes.

REFERENCES

Bandler, R.J., Madaras, G.R., and Bem, D.J. 1968. Self-observation as a source of pain perception. *Journal of Personality and Social Psychology* 9:205-209.

Bem, D.J. 1965. An experimental analysis of self-persuasion. *Journal of Experimental Social Psychology* 1:199-218.

----. 1966. Inducing belief in false confessions. *Journal of Personality and Social Psychology* 3:707-710.

----. 1967. Self-perception: an alternative interpretation of cognitive dissonance phenomena. *Psychological Review* 74:183-200.

Jones, R.A., Linder, D.E., Kiesler, C.A., Zanna, M., and Brehm, J.W. 1968. Internal states or external stimuli: Observers' attitude judgments and the dissonance theory--self-persuasion controversy. *Journal of Experimental Social Psychology* 4:247-269.

Kelley, H.H. 1967. Attribution theory in social psychology. *Nebraska Symposium on Motivation,* Vol. 15, 192-238.

Leventhal, H. 1970. Findings and theory in the study of fear communications. *In* Berkowitz, L. (ed.), *Advances in Experimental Social Psychology,* Vol. 5. New York: Academic Press.

Leventhal, H., Brown, D.H., and Klemp, G.O. 1972. Comparison of the psychological stress properties of AC and DC currents. Manuscript, University of Wisconsin.

Lykken, D.T. 1959. Properties of electrodes used in electrodermal measurement. *Journal of Comparative and Physiological Psychology* 52:629-634.

Mowrer, O.H., and Vieck, P. 1948. An experimental analogue of fear from a sense of helplessness. *Journal of Abnormal and Social Psychology* 43:193-200.

Pervin, L.A. 1963. The need to predict and control under conditions of threat. *Journal of Personality* 31: 570-587.

Piliavin, J.A., Piliavin, I.M., Lowenton, E.P., McCauley, C., and Hammond, P. 1969. On observers' reproductions of dissonance effects: The right answers for the wrong reasons? *Journal of Personality and Social Psychology* 13:98-106.

Stevens, S.S., Carter, A.S., and Shickman, G.M. 1958.

A scale of apparent intensity of electric shock. *Journal of Experimental Psychology* 56:328-344.
Weiss, J.M. 1968. Effects of coping responses on stress. *Journal of Comparative and Physiological Psychology* 65:251-260.
Winer, B.J. 1962. *Statistical Principles in Experimental Design*. New York: McGraw-Hill.

13

Leonard Berkowitz and
Charles Turner

Perceived Anger Level, Instigating Agent, and Aggression

As a further test of the senior author's analysis of purposive aggression, an experiment was carried out extending an earlier study by Berkowitz, Lepinski and Angulo (1969). Eighty university men were moderately provoked by one of the experimenter's two confederates and then were exposed to different treatments in a 4 x 2 factorial design: (a) in three groups they were led to believe that they had either low, medium or high anger towards their tormentor, while no such feedback was provided in the fourth group; (b) they were required to give shocks to another person, either the confederate who had provoked them or the neutral confederate. In accord with the prediction that the subjects' perception of their anger level would influence their aggression only towards the person they thought had aroused this anger in them, the anger-level feedback was related to intensity of aggression only when the frustrater was the available target. Berkowitz's analysis is contrasted with Schachter's (1964) cognitive theory of emotions which deals only with the aroused person's understanding of his feelings and not with the perceived cause of this arousal (except as this cause contributes to the interpretation of the inner sensations). A distinction is drawn between purposive and impulsive aggression, with the latter being governed by associative factors to a much greater extent.

A number of psychologists have recently offered variations of the old James-Lange theory of emotions in attempting to account for emotional reactions. Contrary to common sense, this classic doctrine maintains that the subjective emotional state is the consequence, rather than the cause, of the individual's first response to the arousing situation. We are afraid, the well-worn and oversimplified formula tells us, because we run. Until its recent resurrection, the James-Lange theory had been cast into limbo by Cannon's (1929) criticism of its emphasis on visceral changes. Cannon's arguments cannot fault the contemporary modifications, however, which stress the crucial role played by other response processes, especially cognitions, in determining emotional experiences and actions.

Schachter's cognitive theory (1964) is probably the most familiar version of this new wave of ideas. What the individual specifically feels and how he acts in the instigating situation supposedly depends upon his understanding of his internal sensations. He first experiences some diffuse, undifferentiated arousal, interprets this stirred-up state "in terms of the characteristics of the precipitating situation and his apperceptive mass," and then acts in a manner consistent with this interpretation. The external situation is important here only to the extent that it creates the initial arousal and then helps shape the person's interpretation of his feelings.

Other theorists have gone beyond Schachter's conception by postulating determinants other than the individual's understanding of his bodily sensations. Lazarus, for example (Lazarus, Averill, and Opton, 1968), suggested that the cognitive appraisal governing emotional behavior is influenced by the feedback from the "interplay between the conditions causing an emotion and the effects of efforts to cope with them." External conditions and the person's reactions to them presumably also affect emotional behavior. Bandler, Madaras, and Bem (1968) have also discussed the influence of responses to the environment. They reported that the subjects' judgments of the painfulness of a stimulus were determined by their observations of their own reactions to this stimulus.

The senior author has also referred to this kind of self-observation in his analysis of "purposive aggression." Departing from the strictly cognitive formulations, he has argued that impulsive aggression must be differentiated from deliberate, intentional attacks upon some target (Berkowitz, 1965). Where the latter are goal-oriented and greatly influenced by tactical and strategic considerations, impulsive acts are automatic, stimulus-elicited responses to the external situation governed primarily by associative factors and relatively unaffected by cognitive processes (other than those involved in labeling the environmental stimuli). Focusing on purposive aggression then, Berkowitz (1965:321-322) hypothesized that aggressive desires can develop as the aroused person draws a connection between his internal reactions and some external event, object, or person. To illustrate, suppose this individual is ready to act aggressively for one reason or another and then encounters stimuli in his environment which evoke aggressive as well as other, correlated, reactions from him. He may become aware of his reactions; he notes his motor responses (perhaps his clenched fists), his hostile thoughts, and his visceral changes and may interpret these reactions as "anger". This self-understanding may facilitate aggressive behavior--among other ways, by momentarily heightening the person's set to respond aggressively, by establishing a filtering screen interfering with nonaggressive responses, and by interfering with his detection of nonaggressive stimuli in the situation--but is theoretically not enough to make the person want to attack a specific target. He must posit a causal connection between these "anger" reactions and some specific object in his environment if he is to want to aggress against that particular target. In other words, where Schachter's analysis deals only with processes leading a person to feel angry, we suggest that the person must believe that a certain individual has made him angry if he is to develop an aggressive purpose, that is, intend to injure that individual.

Support for this reasoning can be found in at least two experiments. The first of these, carried out by Valins (1966), has to do with cognitive effects on sexual preferences. Male subjects who were led to believe that their hearts had reacted markedly to certain slides of nude women developed the greatest liking and strongest preference for these particular slides. Although stimulated by Schachter's theory, Valins' study is relevant to the present conception. His men had a specific sexual goal: they wanted certain photos more than others--the pictures that they believed had affected them internally.

A preliminary experiment by Berkowitz, Lepinski, and Angulo (1969) applied the senior author's argument to aggressive behavior. In this study, male university students were induced to believe that a moderately obnoxious peer had made them either highly, moderately, or only slightly angry. These cognitions then influenced the strength of the subjects' subsequent attacks on their peer. The strongest aggression was displayed by the men led to think they were moderately angry with their tormentor, while the supposedly highly angry students evidently had restrained their attacks upon their peer, presumably because they regarded their strong anger toward him as inappropriate in this situation.

The present investigation[1] is addressed to two problems inherent in this earlier experiment. For one, since the insulting treatment was verbally administered in the Berkowitz-Lepinski-Angulo study and there was no appropriate reference scale for judging the harshness of this provocation, we have only an equivocal basis for describing the insult as moderate. Instead of being verbally assaulted, the men in the present study were aroused by giving them a medium number of electric shocks. If this treatment (as well as the one used by Berkowitz, Lepinski, and Angulo) was indeed moderately provoking, the subjects in this experiment should also show a curvilinear relationship between their ostensible anger level and the strength of their subsequent attacks on their tormentor--and again, the men believing themselves moderately angry with their partner should exhibit the strongest aggression towards him.

More importantly, the earlier study did not investiage the goal-directedness of the instigation created by the anger-level information; the subjects could attack only their frustrater. We do not have any definite evidence that they specifically wanted to hurt this person and not someone else, as the senior author's formulation maintains. They might have aggressed against any available target to the same degree because all they were responding to was their interpretation of their feelings. Two targets were therefore provided in this experiment. The subjects in one condition could attack their tormentor, while for the men in another group the potential victim was a stranger. The subjects' anger level should primarily affect their desire to attack the person who, they believed, had aroused this anger in them, and thus the relation between their supposed anger level and the intensity of their aggression should hold only when the subjects were confronting their frustrater.

METHOD

Subjects

Eighty university men, recruited from introductory psychology classes, were distributed among the eight conditions of the 2 x 4 factorial design. Their service in the experiment was in partial fulfillment of their course requirement. Eleven other subjects also participated in the study but were discarded because of suspiciousness (two cases), procedural problems (four cases), or because they had exhibited unusually aggressive behavior from the outset (five cases). Four discarded cases were in the high anger-frustration condition and three in the no feedback-neutral person group. None were in the medium-anger group.

When each subject came to the laboratory at the assigned time, he was met by the experimenter and two other men (supposedly fellow subjects but actually the experimenter's accomplices). The experimenter explained that the study was concerned with "relationships between physiological variables and various aspects of social learning and social perception." The three of them, he said, would be engaged in different tasks in order to get as much information as possible about these interrelationships. He then told the men electric shocks would be used in the experiment and that they could withdraw from the study with full credit if they desired.

After this introduction, the experimenter selected one of the confederates ("Mr. Hunter") apparently randomly, and asked him to go with him to the next room where he would work on his assigned tasks. A few minutes later, the experimenter returned and gave the remaining two men, the subject and the second accomplice ("Mr. Overton"), the instructions for their first assignment. This part would deal with the influence of punishment on social performance, he explained, and various physiological measures would be recorded simultaneously. One of the men would be the "problem solver" who would have five minutes to come up with five ideas for a promotional campaign for a recording artist. The other subject would have to evaluate these ideas by giving him from one to ten shocks, one shock if the ideas were thought to be very good and ten shocks if they were judged to be very bad.

The experimenter chose the confederate, "Overton," again supposedly randomly, to be the evaluator, while the subject was to be the problem solver. The experimenter took the accomplice to another room, and then returned to attach some supposed autonomic sensing devices to the subject--identified as galvanic skin response electrodes and an oncometer for measuring heart rate as well as blood pressure variations in the fingers. He also placed the electric shock electrodes on the same arm. When these were attached, the subject was informed that he had five minutes to write down his five ideas on the assigned problem. The experimenter would leave, he said, but he would talk to the subject over the loudspeaker in the room and let him know when he was to read his ideas to the evaluator, Mr. Overton, who would hear them in his own room. The subject was reminded that he would receive from one to ten shocks, and the experimenter left. At the end of the five-minute work period, the subject was told to read his five ideas. In all conditions, he then received five electric shocks as Overton's supposed evaluation of his solutions.

Experimental Manipulations

The experimental manipulations began upon the experimenter's return, with the first one being the "anger feedback" variation. Subjects in three of the four conditions created along this dimension received misleading information about their anger level following the procedure employed by Berkowitz, Lepinski, and Angulo (1969). The experimenter said that the GSR, heart rate, and blood pressure measurements obtained from the subject would be integrated by the "psychoautonomic integrator" (an imposing box full of dials, switches and wires) in front of him, and that one of the meters would show the subject how angry he was, "much as a lie detector can tell whether a person is lying or not."

As in the earlier study, the experimenter turned on a tape recorder at this point, explaining that further instructions were on tape in order to save time, and again left the room. A taped voice directed the subject's attention to the "anger meter" featured prominently on the "psychoautonomic integrator." He was to write down the meter reading each time he reacted to the stimulus called out to him. The voice then read a list of concepts one at a time: home state, field of psychology, favorite professor, the other subject whom he had just encountered (i.e., Overton), the experimenter. Following the earlier procedure, the subject's dial readings for each of these concepts except "the other subject" always fluctuated below 1, signifying very low anger. The three anger feedback conditions differed in the level of anger the subject supposedly felt toward the person who had given him the five electric shocks. In the low-anger group, the meter readings varied between 0.5 and 1, were between 2.2 and 2.75 in the medium-anger condition, and fluctuated between 4 and 4.2 in the high-anger group. (The highest possible reading was 5.) The men in the fourth condition (no feedback group) were asked to think of the various concepts but were not given any information about their ostensible anger level.

When the experimenter returned, he informed the subject, as in the Berkowitz-Lepinski-Angulo study, that his new job would be to serve as a teacher while his partner tried to learn a particular code using the information given him. One set of lights on the second apparatus situated near the subject would signal whether the partner (the learner) had made a right or wrong response on each trial of the learning task. Being the teacher, the subject was to punish the learner each time he made a mistake and [as in the Buss (1961) "aggression machine" procedure] was to select the shock intensity he thought best for teaching the other person that his answer was incorrect. The subject could select one of ten different shock intensities, ranging from 1 (very low) to a much stronger, though nonharmful, intensity of 10.

The second experimental manipulation, new to the present study, involved the identity of the learner. For half of the subjects in each of the four conditions created up to this point, the learner was said to be Mr. Overton, the person who had evaluated the subject in the previous phase. These men therefore had an opportunity to hurt the individual who had supposedly aroused the given level of anger in them, or who, in the no-feedback group, had provoked them. For the remaining subjects, however, the learner was Mr. Hunter, the accomplice who had left the room in the early minutes of the session. The potential victim in these cases, then, was not the person who had created the given level of anger in them.

Dependent Variables

Repeating the procedure of the Berkowitz-Lepinski-Angulo investigation, the learner was said to be incorrect on 14 of the 20 trials. The primary aggression measure was the mean intensity of the shock administered to the learner in each of four blocks of trial (1-4, 5-8, 10-12, and 14, 15, 17), and over all trials. The duration of each shock was also recorded, but since no significant results were obtained with this measure, nothing more will be said about it here.

The experimenter returned at the completion of the learning task and administered three questionnaires. One of these, as in the earlier study, was the 24-item Nowlis Mood Questionnaire (Nowlis, 1965) which consisted of eight 3-item clusters. In responding to each item, the subject was to check the extent to which the adjective characterized his present mood on a 5-point scale ranging from "definitely applies" to "definitely does not apply." The analyses carried out on this instrument employed the cluster scores. In addition, the subject was also asked, on a second form, to rate his anger after he had been evaluated ("On a scale of ten, how would you rate your mood after the other subject's evaluation of your work?"), and then, on the third questionnaire which supposedly would go to the Psychology Department, to evaluate the experiment and the experimenter. None of the five items on this latter instrument yielded any significant condition differences and these last-mentioned measures will also be ignored in this report.

RESULTS

Manipulation of Perceived Anger Level

Although the three items in the "angry" cluster (angry-defiant-rebellious) of the Nowlis Mood scale did not produce any significant effects, reliable condition differences were obtained with the separate rating of felt anger described above. The analysis of variance revealed a significant main effect for the anger level variation ($F = 2.99$, 3 and 72, *df*, $p = .04$) and no other significant terms. Two points can be raised regarding the mean anger ratings shown in Table 13.1. First, the men in the three feedback conditions evidently felt angrier than the subjects in the no-feedback control group at the time they had been "evaluated" and/or when they had completed the rating. Since all conditions had actually received the same treatment, of course, these differences undoubtedly stem from the perceived anger-level manipulation. Unlike the control subjects, the men in the feedback groups were reminded that they were angry with the person who had shocked them earlier. Thinking of their feelings toward him and the abuse they had received at his hands, they could have stimulated themselves to heightened or persistent anger, where the control subjects had "cooled off" in the intervening minutes. We may recover much more quickly from insults we have received if we do not think of our feelings and refrain from labeling them as "anger."

Second, the reported anger in the three feedback groups generally corresponds with the meter readings. Combining the two target conditions, the subjects informed that they had a low level of anger reported the lowest anger mood, while the men in the high-anger group gave themselves the highest anger ratings. Both the medium- and high-anger conditions differed significantly from the no-feedback group.

TABLE 13.1. Condition Means on Separate Self-Rating of Anger.

	Feedback Conditions				
Target	*Low Anger*	*Medium Anger*	*High Anger*	*No Feedback*	*All Groups*
Frustrater	3.7_{ab}	4.8_{b}	4.2_{ab}	2.5_{a}	3.8
Neutral Person	3.6_{ab}	3.6_{ab}	5.0_{b}	3.0_{ab}	3.8
Combined	3.65_{AB}	4.20_{B}	4.65_{B}	2.75_{A}	

Note: The higher the score, the greater the remembered anger on the 10-point scale. Cells not having a subscript in common are significantly different, by Duncan Multiple Range Test, at the 0.05 level. Cells having lower case subscripts should be compared only with other cells having lower case subscripts.

Aggressive Behavior

Two significant effects were obtained in the analysis of variance of the shock intensity scores, as can be seen in Table 13.2. Of lesser interest is the significant Trials term: As is often found with the Buss procedure, the angry subjects administered ever stronger shocks to their victim from the first trial block to the last (the means are 3.1, 4.5, 4.7, and 5.2 on the 10-point shock intensity scale). More important, the significant effect for Anger Level indicates that the information about their anger level had influenced the subjects' aggressive behavior.

The pattern of results, given in Table 13.3, is generally in accord with our theoretical expectations. When the subjects were attacking their frustrater, the procedure followed in the Berkowitz-Lepinski-Angulo experiment, the strongest aggression was displayed by the men led to believe they had a medium anger level--as was also the case in the earlier study. These people gave their tormentor significantly stronger punishment than was given him in the high-anger and no-feedback groups. By contrast, and also as expected, there was no significant relationship between the subjects' supposed anger level and their subsequent aggression when their target was not the person who had aroused them. There were no reliable differences among the four means in this latter condition.

TABLE 13.2. Analyses of Variance of Shock Intensity Scores.

Source *Between Ss*	*df*	*MS*	*F*	*p*
A. Targets	1	13.31	1.84	
B. Anger Levels	3	39.57	5.47	< .01
A X B	3	7.72	1.07	
Error	72	7.23		
Within Ss				
D. Trials	3	64.59	38.21	<.001
D X A	3	0.70		
D X B	9	0.78		
D X A X B	9	1.72	1.02	
Error	216	1.69		

Our theoretical predictions were also tested by means of trend tests within both the frustrater-victim and neutral person-victim conditions, using only the three feedback groups. The results are given in Table 13.4. As can be seen, the three groups given information about their anger level yielded a significant linear trend, as well as the expected significant quadratic trend, when the frustrater was the aggression victim. There were no reliable trends, on the other hand, as we had also expected, when the subjects were attacking someone who had not provoked them.[2] Their understanding of their anger state affected their deliberate aggressive behavior primarily when they were dealing with the person who had aroused this anger.

TABLE 13.3. Condition Means on Shock Intensity Scores.

	Feedback Conditions				
Target	*Low Anger*	*Medium Anger*	*High Anger*	*No Feedback*	*All Groups*
Frustrater	4.47_{ab}	5.43_{b}	3.29_{a}	3.55_{a}	4.18
Neutral Person	5.08_{b}	4.94_{b}	4.24_{ab}	4.11_{ab}	4.59
Combined	4.77_{A}	5.19_{A}	3.76_{B}	3.83_{B}	

Note: Cells not having a subscript in common are significantly different, by Duncan Multiple Range Test, at the 0.05 level. Cells having lower case subscripts should be compared only with other cells having lower case subscripts.

TABLE 13.4. Trend Analysis of Shock Intensity Data in the Frustrater-Victim and Neutral Person-Victim Conditions.

Source	*df*	*MS*	*F*	*p*
Frustrater Condition	(2)	(45.90)	(6.96)	$<.01$
Linear	1	27.61	4.19	$<.05$
Quadratic	1	64.19	9.74	$<.005$
Neutral Person Condition	(2)	(8.06)	1.22	
Linear	1	13.94	2.11	
Quadratic	1	2.17	0.33	
Error	54	6.59		

Mood Results

We now have to face the question of why the subjects in the high-anger group had not given the frustrater the strongest punishment. Berkowitz, Lepinski, and Angulo had explained their similar results by suggesting that the people in the high-anger condition had regarded their strong anger as inappropriate, considering the relatively moderate provocation, had become anxious, and had suppressed their aggressive inclinations. Their responses to one of the Nowlis Mood clusters appeared to be indicative of their anxiety; they had rated themselves as feeling more sluggish, drowsy, and tired than the subjects in the other conditions. Not caring to admit their "inappropriate" and "bad" emotional state, they could not acknowledge their anxiety explicitly, but did show their tension and concern somewhat indirectly in these fatigue feelings reminiscent of neurasthenic anxiety.

Although this anxiety mood cluster did not lead to any significant effects in the analysis of variance of these data in the present experiment, a closer examination of the condition means was justified by the earlier findings and the clear theoretical prediction. We expected the high-anger group to report the strongest anxiety mood regardless of the nature of their victim; their intense anger was inappropriate because of the moderate insult given them and not because of their potential target--the anxiety presumably arose before they had the opportunity to attack this person--although the presence of the neutral victim might make them more conscious of the inappropriateness of their intense emotion. One-tailed t tests were therefore made comparing the high-anger group mean with each of the other means. The results are summarized in Table 13.5 and, by and large, are in accord with our expectations. Combining the two target conditions, the subjects led to think they were highly angry with their tormentor rated themselves as more anxiously fatigued than the men in the other groups. The difference between this group and the no-feedback control condition achieved significance ($p < .02$) and approached significance in the case of the other means ($p < .07$). Feeling anxious, then, these subjects evidently restrained their attacks on the learner even when he had been the person who had angered them earlier.

DISCUSSION

The present results generally support the senior author's cognitive analysis of purposive aggression. Emotionally aroused people seek to attack a particular target when (a) they interpret their internal sensations as "anger," and (b) they believe this specific target had been the

TABLE 13.5. Condition Means on Anxiety Mood Measure (Sluggish-Drowsy-Tired).

	Feedback Conditions			
Target	*Low Anger*	*Medium Anger*	*High Anger*	*No Feedback*
Frustrater	7.9	7.8	8.3	7.7
Neutral Person	8.4	8.2	10.7	7.0
Combined	8.1	8.0	9.5	7.3

Note: The higher the score, the greater the anxiety mood. The high-anger group mean, 9.5, is significantly different from the no-feedback mean, 7.3, by one-tailed t test ($p < .02$) and is nearly significantly different from the other means ($p < .07$).

cause of their feelings. As indicated in this study, the intensity of the subjects' desire to hurt a particular person, reflected in the intensity of the punishment given him, arose from their perceptions of the strength of their anger and their belief that this person had been the one who had provoked them. Looked at from a larger perspective, the findings also provide yet another demonstration of the search for cognitive consistency. We want our actions to be in accord with our emotions, as we understand them, and apparently we are also disturbed if these feelings do not seem to be warranted by the causal incident. The emotion as well as the behavior must be consistent with our other cognitions.

This cognitive analysis does not contend that all aggression follows this formula. As noted in the introductory section, Berkowitz has repeatedly also pointed to the role of associative factors in aggression. Stimuli in the environment that are associated with aggressive behavior generally, such as nearby weapons, can evoke aggressive responses from people who are ready to attack someone (Berkowitz and LePage, 1967), and the available target's connection with the victim of other, recently observed violent actions also influences the strength of the attacks upon this target (see, for example, Geen and Berkowitz, 1966). One of the important tasks facing the study of emotional reactions is to isolate the conditions governing the operation of these two causal processes. When do associative factors dominate and when do cognitive determinants become relatively more important?

NOTES

1. This experiment was carried out under Grant GS-1228 from the National Science Foundation to Leonard Berkowitz. We are indebted to Mr. David Singer for the skill and care with which he carried out this research.

2. If the Frustrater and Neutral Person target conditions are combined, the trend analysis reveals significant linear and quadratic trends for Anger Level ($p < .05$) and a near significant quadratic interaction of Anger Level by Available Target ($F = 3.24$, 1 and 54 *df*, $p < .10$). The clear theoretical prediction, we believe, justifies the testing of condition differences as summarized in Tables 13.3 and 13.4.

REFERENCES

Bandler, R.J., Madaras, G.R., and Bem, D.J. 1968. Self-observation as a source of pain perception. *Journal of Personality and Social Psychology* 9:205-209.

Berkowitz, L. 1965. The concept of aggressive drive: Some additional considerations. *In* L. Berkowitz (ed.), *Advances in Experimental Social Psychology*, Vol. 2. New York: Academic Press, 301-329.

Berkowitz, L., and LePage, A. 1967. Weapons as aggression-eliciting stimuli. *Journal of Personality and Social Psychology* 7:202-207.

Berkowitz, L., Lepinski, J., and Angulo, E. 1969. Awareness of own anger level and subsequent aggression. *Journal of Personality and Social Psychology* 11:293-300.

Buss, A. 1961. *The Psychology of Aggression*. New York: Wiley.

Cannon, W.B. 1929. *Bodily Changes in Pain, Hunger, Fear and Rage* (Second ed.). New York: Appleton.

Geen, R.G., and Berkowitz, L. 1966. Name-mediated aggressive cue properties. *Journal of Personality* 34: 456-465.

Lazarus, R.S., Averill, J.B., and Opton, E.M., Jr. 1968. *Towards a cognitive theory of emotion*. Paper given at Symposium on Feelings and Emotion, October 11-13, Loyola University, Chicago, Ill.

Nowlis, V. 1965. Research with the mood adjective check list. *In* S. S. Tompkins and C. Izard (eds.), *Affect, Cognition, and Personality*. New York: Springer, 352-389.

Schachter, S. 1964. The interaction of cognitive and physiological determinants of emotional state. *In* L. Berkowitz (ed.), *Advances in Experimental Social Psychology*, Vol 1. New York: Academic Press, 49-80.

Valins, S. 1966. Cognitive effects of false heart-rate feedback. *Journal of Personality and Social Psychology* 4:400-408.

14

Richard E. Nisbett and
Michael D. Storms

Cognitive and Social Determinants of Food Intake

Three experiments are reported, all of which tested the hypothesis that the food intake of overweight individuals is more affected by external cues of a cognitive or social nature than is the food intake of individuals who are not overweight. All of the experiments indicate that the food intake of people in general is affected by cognitive and social cues, but none of them indicate that overweight individuals are more responsive to such cues than other individuals. On the contrary, one of the experiments indicates that the eating behavior of overweight individuals is under less cognitive control than is that of normal individuals. It was suggested that overweight individuals may be highly responsive only to external cues of a sensory nature and that the differences between the eating behavior of normal and obese individuals have their origin in biological processes rather than labelling processes.

Considerable research has recently been conducted testing Schachter's hypothesis that overweight individuals are unresponsive to "internal," physiological cues signalling hunger and satiety and highly responsive to "external," food- or environment-related cues. Several studies give strong support to the contention that overweight individuals are unresponsive to internal cues. Their food intake is relatively unaffected by prior consumption of food, or by fear, which mimics satiety signals (Schachter, Goldman, and Gordon, 1968); their verbal report of hunger is relatively unrelated to the length of time since their last meal (Nisbett, 1968a), or to the degree of gastric motility they are experiencing (Stunkard and Koch, 1964); and their impulse buying in supermarkets does not increase with deprivation as it does for normal individuals (Nisbett and Kanouse, 1969).

Evidence that the obese are more responsive to external cues is extensive but circumscribed. Initial definitions of the concept of an external cue were quite broad (e.g., Schachter, 1967; Nisbett, 1968a), encompassing the sensory properties of food, cognitions about food and hunger, and social cues which encourage or inhibit eating. By now, a considerable amount of research has demonstrated that the obese are indeed highly responsive to sensory food cues. In several studies, the obese have been shown to eat more good food and/or less bad food than normal subjects (Hashim and Van Itallie, 1965; Nisbett, 1968a, in press), and the obese have been shown to be highly motivated to eat by the sight of food (Mayer, Monello, and Seltzer, 1965; Nisbett, 1968b; Ross, 1969; Johnson, 1970).

In contrast, there is little evidence that the obese are more responsive to external cues which are not sensory in nature. Schachter and Gross (1968) have reported that the obese eat more when persuaded by a rigged clock that it is mealtime. Aside from that study, there are no published reports on the effects of any other cognitive or social cues on the food intake of normal and obese subjects. A wider sampling of external cues would appear to be in order.

The present series of studies[1] examines the response of overweight and normal subjects to a variety of cognitive and social cues. The first experiment tests the hypothesis that overweight individuals are more affected by a social facilitation manipulation than are normal individuals. The second experiment tests the hypothesis that overweight individuals are more affected by purely cognitive, experimenter-supplied information about deprivation state than are normal individuals. The third experiment tests the hypothesis that overweight individuals are more affected by implicit, socially supplied definitions of appropriate meal size. The third experiment also examines the degree to which overweight individuals maintain conscious surveillance of the amount of food they are consuming.

EXPERIMENT I

Method

Overview. The first experiment was designed to determine whether the overweight are more responsive than normal individuals to social cues which facilitate or discourage eating. Subjects were invited to participate in an investigation of correlates of ability to taste "phenylcinnamaldehyde," a fictional substance allegedly similar to PTC (phenylthiocarbamide) in that "ability to detect its bitter taste is genetically determined." Subjects were shown a bowl of crackers allegedly impregnated with PCM and were asked to taste the crackers in order to determine whether they could detect the PCM. Some subjects ate alone while others ate in the company of an experimental confederate. In one condition, the confederate ate a large number of crackers, and in another condition, he ate only one cracker. The experiment makes it possible to examine the number of crackers eaten as a function of social circumstances and the subjects' weight.

Procedure. Subjects participated either at an afternoon session (between 4:00 and 5:00) or an evening session (between 9:00 and 10:00). At the recruitment telephone call, subjects were asked not to snack after lunch if they were to participate in the afternoon, or after dinner if they were to participate in the evening. This instruction was intended to insure that subjects would be somewhat food deprived and therefore be willing to eat crackers. On arrival at the experiment, subjects were told that physical and social correlates of PCM tasting were being examined. Two points were emphasized in order to leave subjects free to eat as many or as few crackers as they wanted. 1) In order to prevent subjects from eating several crackers in a vain attempt to taste the fictitious PCM, they were told that the ability to taste PCM was a dichotomous rather than a continuous variable. "In other words, if you are a 'taster,' you will taste it clearly and unambiguously. The crackers will taste quite bitter to you. If you are a 'nontaster,' that, too will be clear and unambiguous, and you will taste only the normal flavoring of the cracker." 2) In order to encourage subjects to eat as many crackers as they wanted if the crackers did not taste bitter to them, the experimenter said: "As we asked you not to eat since your last regularly scheduled meal, please feel free to eat as many crackers as you want." Since the crackers did not in fact have a bitter taste this meant that all subjects were free to eat. These instructions completed, the experimenter asked the subject to fill out a questionnaire on physical traits and demographic characteristics after determining whether or not he could taste the PCM.

Manipulating Social Cues. (1) In the Social Facilitation condition, the subject participated with a confederate whose arrival at the laboratory was timed to match that of the subject. The confederate and subject were asked not to speak to each other at any point in order to avoid the possibility of their influencing each other. After completing his instructions, the experimenter left subject and confederate to complete the experimental task together. The confederate ate one entire cracker, then began answering the questionnaire. He ate a total of ten crackers at a rapid pace during the first three minutes, roughly the time required to finish one page of the questionnaire. He then ate ten more crackers at a slower pace, about one every 45 seconds.

(2) In the Social Suppression condition, subjects participated with a confederate who ate only the minimal amount necessary to fulfill the experimental obligation--a single cracker. He then silently filled out a questionnaire.

(3) In the Alone condition, subjects participated by themselves with no confederate present.

Subjects. Subjects for this experiment as well as for Experiments II and III were undergraduate male students at Yale University. Subjects in all three experiments were defined as overweight if their weight was 15% or more over the average for their height (Metropolitan Life Insurance Company, 1959). Subjects were defined as normal if their deviation from average weight was within $\pm$ 5%. Subjects were defined as underweight if their weight was 7% or more under the average. In each experiment, subjects were screened so as to invite only those students whose college records indicated that they were clearly overweight, underweight, or close to the middle of the normal range.

Results

It was anticipated that, compared with the baseline of the Alone condition, the Social Facilitation condition would increase intake and the Social Suppression condition would decrease intake. To the extent that obese individuals are unusually responsive to social stimuli, their eating behavior should be more affected by the social circumstances than that of nonobese individuals. Figure 14.1 presents grams of crackers eaten as a function of weight and experimental condition. It may be seen that the effect of the social situation was quite large ($F = 7.85$, $p < .01$).[2] Subjects in all three weight groups ate more in the Social Facilitation condition than their counterparts in the Alone condition, and overweight and normal subjects ate more in the Alone condition than in the Social Suppression condition. Overweight subjects were not more affected by the manipulation than other subjects. The *F* for the interaction of weight with treatment is less than 1.

The data show that social cues, at least in the eating situation of Experiment I, are important determinants of intake.[3] There is no indication, however, that overweight individuals are more responsive to social cues than other individuals.

EXPERIMENT II

The second experiment was designed to test the hypothesis that the food intake of the obese is affected by externally supplied information about internal state. An attempt was made to influence intake by giving subjects false information about deprivation state.

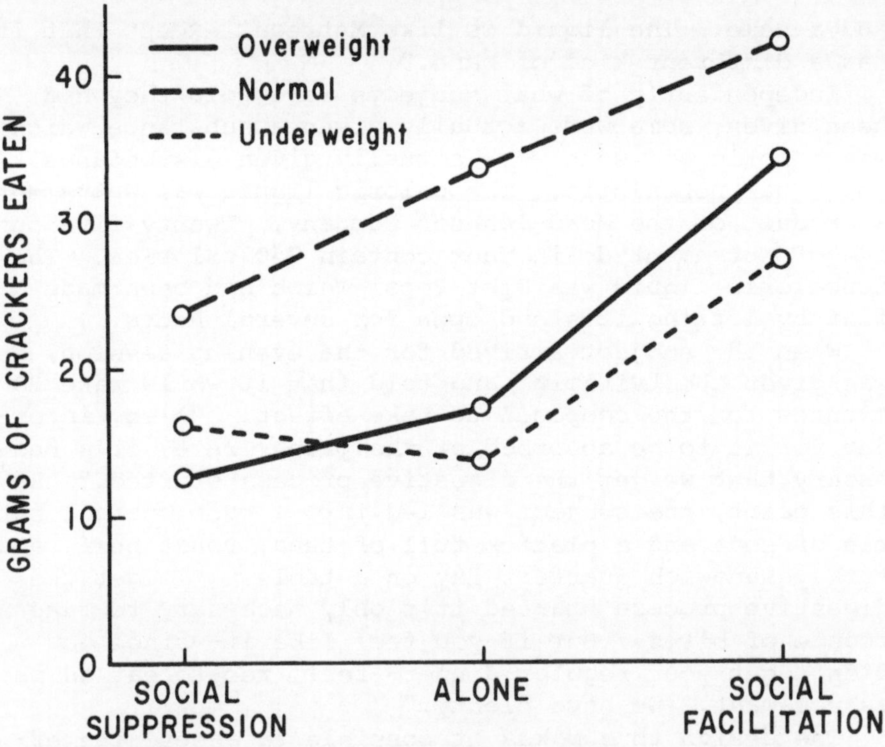

FIGURE 14.1. Grams of crackers eaten as a function of weight and social cues. $N = 10$ for each point.

Method

Subjects were invited to participate in a two-session experiment on the effect of a vitamin compound on memory power. At an afternoon "baseline" session, they were given a brief memory test and then told that it was essential that they not eat dinner before the evening experimental session (scheduled for a time between 6 and 9 p.m.) because the effects of the vitamin compound which they would be given at that time depended on the state of the digestive system. Subjects were given 25 ounces of a liquid which they were asked to drink two hours before the evening session. Some of the subjects were told that the liquid was a lining substance which would help control the absorption rate of the vitamin compound. The liquid was described to other subjects as the equivalent of a 750 calorie meal: "A 750 calorie meal, for example, would be a hamburger, French fries and a coke. The liquid is like Metrecal except that it has a different kind of base."

Independently of what subjects were told they had been given, some were actually given a substance which was caloric and some were actually given a substance which was noncaloric. The caloric liquid was Nutrament, a product of the Mead-Johnson Company. Twenty-five ounces of Nutrament do in fact contain 750 calories. The noncaloric liquid was Diet Pepsi which had been made flat by letting it stand open for several hours.

When the subject arrived for the evening session, he was given the "vitamin" and told that it would take 20 minutes for the compound to take effect. "Also, in order for it to be absorbed at the proper rate, it's necessary that we get the digestive process started." At this point, the subject was led into a room where a bottle of soda and a platter full of tuna, roast beef, and turkey sandwich quarters lay on a table. "To get the digestive process started it's only necessary to take a couple of bites. But if you feel like it--since you didn't get your regular dinner--feel free to eat as much as you want. We have plenty."

The design thus makes it possible to assess the effect of experimenter-supplied information about deprivation state. Some subjects were led to believe that, two hours before they sat down in front of the sandwich platter, they had consumed the equivalent of a 750 calorie meal. Other subjects were led to believe that they had nothing of caloric value since lunchtime, several hours before their opportunity to eat sandwiches. The manipulation of the actual caloric value of the "preload" makes it possible to examine the effect of experimenter-supplied information both when subjects have been deprived and when they have been preloaded with food.

Results

To the extent that overweight individuals are affected by cognitions about internal state--by estimates of how much they have eaten or need to eat--they would be expected to eat more sandwiches when they believe that they are in a state of food deprivation than when they believe that they have recently had the equivalent of a meal. Table 14.1 presents mean number of sandwiches eaten as a function of the information given subjects about the caloric value of the liquid which they drank two hours before the experimental session. Table 14.1 combines data for subjects who actually received a caloric preload and those who actually received a noncaloric preload, since the cognitive manipulation had equivalent effects regardless of the actual nature of the preload ($F < 1$ for interaction between cognitive manipulation and preload manipulation). It may be seen that the cognitive manipulation had small and approximately equal effects on the intake of all three weight groups. The effect of the manipulation is statistically significant ($p < .05$), but the interaction between weight and information condition is trivial; overweight subjects are not more responsive to information about internal state than are other subjects.

TABLE 14.1. Number of Sandwiches Eaten as a Function of Weight and Description of the Caloric Value of the Liquid.

Weight	*Described as Caloric*	*Described as Noncaloric*
Underweight	1.25	1.54
N	(21)	(20)
Normal	1.73	1.81
N	(22)	(17)
Overweight	2.38	2.60
N	(18)	(16)

Note: Dieting subjects ($N = 19$) are not included in this analysis. The pattern is essentially the same when they are included, however.

It should be pointed out that the cognitive manipulation was not accomplished with uniform success. Upon questioning, 13% of the subjects given false information expressed some doubts about the descriptions of the caloric value of the liquid. However, when doubting subjects are removed from the analysis, the conclusions are not altered with respect either to the main effect or to the interaction.

A quite unexpected result was the finding that overweight subjects were fully as responsive to the *actual* caloric value of the preload as were other subjects. Underweight subjects given Nutrament consumed 1.01 sandwiches on the average while underweight subjects given Diet Pepsi consumed 1.76 sandwiches. The comparable figures for normal subjects are 1.59 vs. 1.98 and for overweight subjects 2.10 vs. 2.86. This pattern of data is inconsistent with previous work showing that overweight individuals are less responsive to differences in internal state than are other individuals. In particular, the finding directly conflicts with the Schachter, Goldman, and Gordon (1968) experiment which found that overweight individuals ate as many crackers after they had just eaten two roast beef sandwiches as when they had had nothing to eat for several hours. However, the preload manipulation in that experiment differed from the present manipulation in at least two respects. The preload used by Schachter et al. was a solid instead of liquid food and it was given immediately before the experimental session rather than two hours before. Perhaps overweight individuals are responsive to calories in liquid form, or perhaps they are responsive to a preload after a delay. Experiment III explored the latter possibility by giving subjects a liquid preload immediately before giving them a second opportunity to eat.

With respect to the initial hypothesis, the results of Experiments I and II are clear enough. They indicate that subjects in general are affected both by social and by cognitive cues which facilitate or discourage eating, but neither experiment provides evidence that overweight subjects are any more affected by these cues than are other subjects.

Experiment III

The third experiment used quite different techniques to assess the effects of social and cognitive cues. The social cue employed was an implicit definition of meal size: subjects were served sandwiches either in "meal" form (quarters) or in "snack" form (sixteenths). It was anticipated that subjects in general would believe that it was intended for them to eat more when they were served quarters than when they were served hors d'oeuvre-like sixteenths. Quartered sandwiches on a platter resemble normal luncheon fare and should establish an implicit set for normal lunchtime eating. Hors d'oeuvres on a platter have an entirely different appearance and should establish a set for "polite" snacking. If the overweight are more susceptible to social cues which implicitly define meal size, they should eat less food when it is presented in hors d'oeuvre form.

Experiment III also provided for an assessment of the degree to which subjects maintain cognitive surveillance of food intake. It is possible that overweight individuals regulate their intake cognitively, by counting. If the overweight individual is unable to utilize internal satiety cues in controlling his intake, perhaps he relies on a careful cognitive surveillance of the amount he is consuming. If this is so, one would expect to find that overweight individuals would be more likely to "count" how much they eat, and overweight subjects in Experiment III should be better able to remember how much they have eaten than normal subjects.

Method

Subjects were recruited by telephone to participate in an experiment on the effects of blood-sugar level on memory which was being conducted by the "Yale Food and Drug Institute." Subjects were offered $1.50 and, if they agreed to participate, were scheduled for 10:00 a.m., 11:15 a.m., or 12:30 p.m. on the following day. Subjects were asked not to eat during the three hours immediately before the experiment.

When subjects arrived at the experiment, they were told that the memory task would consist of learning paired nonsense syllables while their blood-sugar level was high and having their memory for the syllables tested while their blood sugar level was low. Subjects were told that their memory of the nonsense syllable pairs was to be tested at 4:00 p.m. that afternoon. "When you take the test at 4:00, I want your blood-sugar level to be low. Since it takes three hours after eating for blood-sugar to drop off to normal, you cannot eat lunch after you leave here. But since it is perfectly safe to eat before you leave here-- that would still give you at least 3 hours before 4:00--I'll offer you some refreshments." Subjects were assured that they did not have to come back to the laboratory at 4:00 p.m. but instead would test themselves and return their results by mail. The actual reason for telling subjects that they could not eat after leaving the laboratory was the fact that it was essential to prevent them from refusing the refreshments on the grounds that they would be going to lunch immediately after the experiment.

Manipulating Deprivation State. Subjects were told: "Of course your blood-sugar is low now; you haven't eaten in three hours. So, to increase your blood-sugar level for the learning task I'll give you this pill (liquid)." At this point half of the subjects were given a placebo pill (Deprived condition) and were thus left in a state of food deprivation, and the other half were given 25 ounces (750 calories) of Nutrament (Preloaded condition). Subjects were then handed a list of paired nonsense syllables to memorize and the experimenter left the room.

Manipulating Definition of Meal Size and Measuring Surveillance. After ten minutes, the experimenter reappeared with a tray of tuna fish salad sandwiches on white bread, a pitcher of water, and a questionnaire. Subjects were told to complete the questionnaire and to help themselves to the refreshments, eating as few or as many as they liked. The experimenter then left the room. Half of the subjects were served four sandwiches cut into quarters (Quarters condition), and half received four sandwiches cut into hors d'oeuvres-like, open-faced sixteenths (Hors d'Oeuvres condition). The questionnaire asked, among several filler items, questions pertaining to subjects' food intake that morning. After 15 minutes, the experimenter reappeared with another short questionnaire and removed the tray of sandwiches. The new questionnaire asked, in addition to filler items, the key question pertaining to surveillance of food intake, "How many individual pieces of sandwich do you think you ate?"

The experiment allows the assessment of the effect of a social cue implying appropriate meal size and the assessment of the degree of conscious surveillance of intake, under conditions both of deprivation and preloading with liquid food. The experiment also makes it possible to pursue the anomalous finding of Experiment II that a liquid preload, given two hours before a second opportunity to eat, suppressed the intake of overweight subjects to the same degree that it suppressed the intake of other subjects. If the equal suppression was due to the long delay between preload and eating opportunity, then the short delay in Experiment III should result in differential suppresion of intake for overweight and normal subjects.

Results

If overweight individuals are highly responsive to socially supplied definitions of meal size, it would be expected that they would eat more food when presented with quarters than when presented with hors d'oeuvres. Figure 14.2 presents grams of sandwiches eaten as a function of the size of the sandwich units and deprivation condition. As a group, subjects consumed more sandwiches in quartered form than in hors d'oeuvre form ($p < .05$). In the Preloaded condition, in which subjects began their eating in a state of relative satiety, the effect of sandwich size was equivalent for obese and normal subjects. In the Deprived condition, however, the pattern is the opposite of that predicted by the social cue hypothesis. Whereas normal and overweight subjects in the Deprived condition ate roughly the same number of sandwiches in quartered form ($t < 1$), overweight subjects ate far more sandwiches in hors d'oeuvre form than normal subjects ($t = 3.37$, $p < .001$). This dramatic difference between overweight and normal subjects in the Deprived condition will be discussed later. For the moment, it is clear that there is not the slightest sign of support for the hypothesis that overweight individuals are more likely than normal individuals to eat little in response to an implicit suggestion that meal size should be small.

The cognitive surveillance hypothesis fares no better. In addition to intake data, Figure 14.2 presents the number of sandwich units (converted into grams) which subjects remembered having eaten immediately after the platter was withdrawn. If overweight subjects regulate their intake cognitively, by counting, then they should be more accurate in their recall than normal subjects.

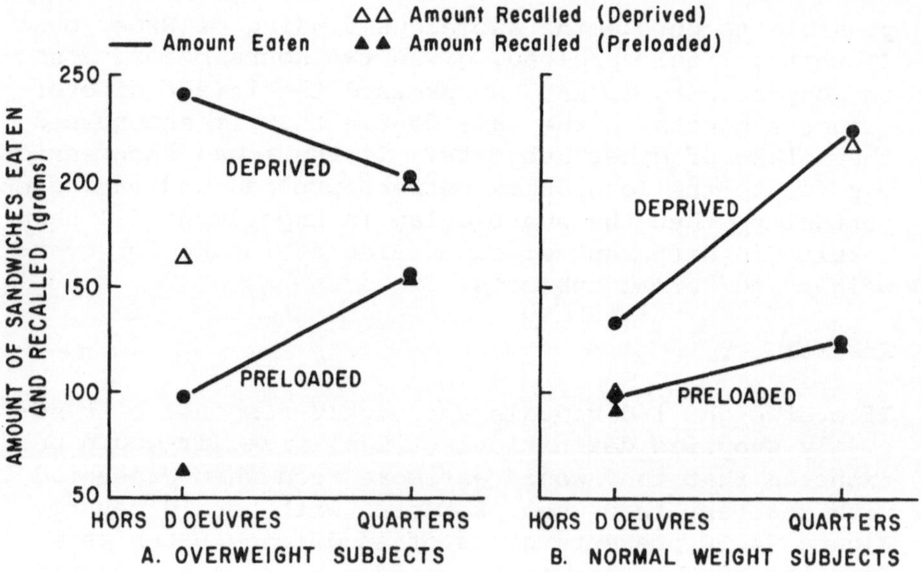

FIGURE 14.2. Amount of sandwiches eaten and amount recalled as a function of deprivation state and size of sandwich units. (a) Data for overweight subjects. (b) Data for normal subjects. *N* = 12 for each condition.

There was little inaccuracy on the part of any of the subjects, normal or obese, who were given sandwich quarters. Subjects given quarters ate approximately three-six quarters and very few subjects misremembered the amount they had eaten. Among subjects given the smaller hors d'oeuvres, however, inaccuracy was frequent--and much more frequent for obese than for normal subjects. Whether inaccuracy is defined as the amount eaten minus the amount recalled, or defined in proportional terms (amount eaten minus amount recalled divided by amount eaten) obese subjects were the less accurate (both *p*'s $< .01$).[4] It is perhaps not surprising that overweight subjects given hors d'oeuvres were highly inaccurate in the Deprived condition: they ate so much (22 hors d'oeuvres on the average) that it would certainly have been difficult to keep track. But overweight subjects given hors d'oeuvres were more inaccurate in the Preloaded condition as well. In that condition they ate almost exactly as much as normal subjects but tended to remember having eaten less. A comparison of proportional errors made by overweight and normal subjects in that condition approaches significance ($t = 2.00$, $p < .07$). These results suggest that, far from regulating his intake by counting, the overweight individual may actually be less aware of the amount of food he is consuming than is the normal individual.

Finally, it should be noted that, as in Experiment II, the intake of overweight subjects was just as much suppressed by the Nutrament preload as was that of normal subjects. This replication suggests that the greater delay in Experiment II was irrelevant and that the marked response to the preload by overweight subjects in both Experiments II and III was due to the fact that the preload was in liquid form. As we will see, this hypothesis has received strong support from an experiment by Pliner (1974).

DISCUSSION

The results concerning the original focus of the investigation may be summarized as follows:

1. Subjects in general consumed more food in the presence of someone who was eating a great deal and less food in the presence of someone who was eating very little. There is no evidence that overweight individuals are any more affected by social cues of this type than are other individuals.

2. Subjects in general were influenced by experimenter-supplied information about nutritional state. When they were told they had previously eaten the equivalent of a small meal they ate slightly less than they did when they were told they had had nothing caloric to eat for several hours. There is no indication that overweight individuals are any more affected by information of this type than are other individuals.

3. Normal individuals consume less when food is given to them in small, snack-size units than when it is given to them in larger, meal-size units. Overweight individuals behave similarly when they have previously been given a large quantity of liquid food, but behave in the opposite way when they are in a state of food deprivation. This finding indicates that, under some circumstances, overweight individuals are less likely

to be affected by implicit social guides to appropriate intake than are normal individuals.

4. When food is given in small units, overweight individuals are less accurate in recalling the number of units they have eaten than are normal individuals. This suggests that overweight individuals do not regulate food intake by counting.

The present experiments show that the food intake of people in general is affected by cognitive and social cues. The present experiments all fail to show that obese individuals are more responsive to such cues than normal individuals. It thus begins to appear likely that, while obese individuals are more responsive to external cues of a sensory nature, this responsiveness may not extend to very many other kinds of external cues.

Despite the negative tenor of this conclusion, the present experiments do pose some interesting puzzles. There is a considerable body of evidence indicating that the obese are less responsive than normals to internal cues, but the obese were found in two of the present studies to be as responsive as normal subjects to liquid preloads. While it is not yet clear why this is the case, it appears to be a reliable, repeatable finding. Pliner (1974) gave obese and normal subjects 600- or 200-calorie preloads in either solid or liquid form and then allowed them to eat sandwiches. Normal bubjects ate fewer sandwiches after the high-calorie than after the low-calorie preload whether the preload was given in solid or in liquid form. Overweight subjects ate just as much after the high-calorie solid preload as after the low-calorie solid preload but ate less after the high-calorie liquid preload than after the low-calorie liquid preload. Her results therefore replicate in the same experiment the finding of Schachter, Goldman, and Gordon (1968) that overweight subjects are unresponsive to solid preloads and the present findings that overweight subjects are highly responsive to liquid preloads. Precisely why obese individuals are responsive to liquid preloads is not at all clear. This exception may prove to be quite useful in understanding the general insensitivity of obese individuals to internal cues.

A second puzzle is presented by the pattern of food intake results in Experiment III. The food intake of normal and overweight subjects in all conditions of Experiment III was essentially identical except for the Deprived condition in which subjects were given hors d'oeuvres. Here the results were dramatically different for normal and overweight subjects. Overweight subjects consumed 82% more than normal subjects in that condition. The results for this condition of the experiment, where the behavior of overweight and normal subjects was so different, require some attempt at explanation. The very large intake of overweight subjects can be understood by taking seriously the implications of the "recall" data: overweight subjects do not monitor their food intake, but instead eat rather inattentively. Overweight subjects in the Deprived condition given hors d'oeuvres were therefore insensitive to the implicit definition of meal size because they were not paying attention to how much they were eating. In the absence of awareness, the attractive sensory cues kept them eating at a high rate. Normal subjects were aware of how much they were eating and stopped when they reached an appropriate "snack" limit. Overweight subjects eating hors d'oeuvres in the Preloaded condition would have been unaware of how much they were eating, but unlike deprived *S*s, would have stopped because satiety cues from the liquid preload supervened.

This post hoc explanation is given added credence by a demonstration made by Ross (1969). Ross allowed both overweight and normal subjects to have access to cashew nuts. During part of the period of access to cashews, Ross directed the attention of subjects to nonfood aspects of their environment. When this was done, normal subjects tended to eat less but overweight subjects tended to eat more. The experiment suggests that, for overweight individuals, eating is a relatively unconscious affair. When their thoughts are directed away from food, they eat more. Similarly, in the present experiment, when a different kind of strain was placed on conscious surveillance of intake (and when satiety cues could not supervene), overweight subjects again ate more.

Finally, it should be noted that the net effect of the present research is to suggest separation of the study of obesity from the general theoretical orientation of the other chapters in this volume. It now appears unlikely that eating behavior of the obese is highly susceptible to cognitive manipulation. While the research on obesity inspired by Schachter grew directly out of research on cognitive and social determinants of the labels which individuals apply to feeling states, it does not appear likely that the errors made by the obese fit into that paradigm. Nisbett (1968b, 1972a, 1972b), Nisbett and Gurwitz (1970), and Schachter (1971) have pointed to the striking parallels which exist between the eating behavior of the rat made obese by lesions of the ventromedial hypothalamus and the eating behavior of the obese human. These parallels suggest that it is a biological process, and not a cognitive or social one, which differentiates the obese from the normal individual.

NOTES

1. The research reported here was supported by Grant 6B 33918 from the National Science Foundation. The authors wish to thank Barney Brawer, Neal Conner, Ted Dushane, Jerry Finch, Andrew Skodol, Claude Thau and Mark Zanna for their assistance in conducting Experiment I.

2. All *p* values reported in this paper are based on two-tailed tests.

3. It may be seen that normal subjects ate more crackers than either overweight subjects or underweight subjects. Crackers, of course, are not a highly attractive food, and subjects had been deprived of food for several hours before the experiment. This combination of external and internal circumstances probably conspired against the frequent tendency which has been observed in eating behavior experiments for overweight subjects to eat more than normal subjects.

4. Measures defining error in terms of the absolute value of the amount eaten minus the amount recalled give almost identical results. Only four normal and two overweight subjects recalled having eaten *more* units than they actually did, and these errors were all quite small.

REFERENCES

Hashim, S., and Van Itallie, T. 1965. Studies in normal and obese subjects with a monitored food-dispens-

ing device. *Annals of the New York Academy of Science* 131:654-661.
Johnson, W.G. 1970. The effect of prior taste and food visibility on the food-directed instrumental performance of the obese. Ph.D. dissertation, Catholic University of America.
Mayer, J., Monello, L., and Seltzer, C. 1965. Hunger and satiety sensations in man. *Postgraduate Medicine* 37:A-97-A-102.
Metropolitan Life Insurance Company. 1959. New weight standards for men and women. *Statistical Bulletin* 40:1-4.
Nisbett, R.E. 1968a. Taste, deprivation and weight determinants of eating behavior. *Journal of Personality and Social Psychology* 10:107-116.
----. 1968b. Determinants of food intake in human obesity. *Science* 159:1254-1255.
----. 1972a. Eating behavior and obesity in men and animals. *Advances in Psychosomatic Medicine* 7:173-193.
----. 1972b. Hunger, obesity and the ventromedial hypothalamus. *Psychological Review* 79:433-453.
Nisbett, R.E., and Gurwitz, S. 1970. Weight, sex and the eating behavior of human newborns. *Journal of Comparative and Physiological Psychology* 73:245-253.
Nisbett, R.E., and Kanouse, D.E. 1969. Obesity, food deprivation and supermarket shopping behavior. *Journal of Personality and Social Psychology* 12:289-294.
Pliner, Patricia. 1974. Internal regulation of food intake by normal and obese subjects as a function of various preloads. Manuscript, University of Toronto.
Ross, L.D. 1969. Cue- and cognition-controlled eating among obese and normal subjects. Ph.D. dissertation, Columbia University.
Schachter, S. 1967. Cognitive effects on bodily functioning: Studies of obesity and eating. *In* D.C. Glass (ed.), *Neurophysiology and Emotion*. New York: Rockefeller University Press and Russell Sage Foundation.
----. 1971. Some extraordinary facts about obese humans and rats. *American Psychologist* 26:129-144.
Schachter, S., Goldman, R., and Gordon, A. 1968. Effects of fear, food deprivation and obesity on eating. *Journal of Personality and Social Psychology* 10:91-97.

Schachter, S., and Gross, L.P. 1968. Manipulated time and eating behavior. *Journal of Personality and Social Psychology* 10:98-106.

Stunkard, A., and Koch, C. 1964. The interpretation of gastric motility. *Archives of General Psychiatry* 11: 74-82.

VI

Discussion

15

Daryl J. Bem

Cognitive Alteration of Feeling States: A Discussion

During the Sixties, it will be recalled, all thinking beings were characterized by chronic drives toward consistency and uncertainty reduction, vigilant forces which coaxed us all toward cognitive quiescence. Our affects, cognitions, and behaviors were held in homeostatic harmony, and our "evaluative needs" initiated emergency information searches whenever any internal state broke through threshold without clear identification or certified cause. In contrast, we are emerging into the Seventies as less driven, more contemplative creatures, thoughtful men and women whose only motivation is the willingness to answer the question "How do you feel?" as honestly and as carefully as possible after calmly surveying the available internal and external evidence.

There is, in short, a shift of paradigm taking place within social psychology, a shift from motivation/drive models of cognitions, behaviors, and feeling states to information processing/attribution models of such phenomena. The chapters in this volume not only reflect and contribute to this shift of paradigm, but they point to some of the "hybrid" theories that will be required if the problems laid bare by the new paradigm are to be solved without "unsolving" some of the problems supposedly laid to rest by the older paradigm.

Four separate lines of research and theory mark this transformation. First, of course, are the various cognitive consistency theories, whose formal history is usually traced to Heider's 1946 article, "Attitudes and Cognitive Organizations" (McGuire, 1966). The system Heider proposed employed the motivational constructs of Gestalt psychology, and he elaborated the theory in the well-known *The Psychology of Interpersonal Relations* (1958), and explored the motivational aspects in a 1960 contribution to the *Nebraska Symposium on Motivation.*

During the decade of the Fifties, several other consistency formulations were developed, and collectively they set the dominant tone of the motivational/drive paradigm during the early Sixties. This era appeared to culminate with the publication of the massive sourcebook of such theories in 1968 (Abelson, Aronson, McGuire, Newcomb, Rosenberg, and Tannenbaum, 1968). The explicit treatment of "feeling states" within this paradigm was provided in *The Cognitive Control of Motivation,* edited and authored by Zimbardo (1969), which applied dissonance-theoretic operations to the manipulation of hunger, thirst, pain, and the like.

The second research tradition involved in the paradigm shift is Schachter's work on the cognitive and physiological foundations of emotional states (Schachter, 1964). Although Schachter's theorizing has not been associated with the cognitive consistency paradigm as such, it is rooted in the same tradition, and the major motivational concept, "evaluative needs," rests upon Festinger's earlier theory of social comparison processes (1954). It is a variant of this motivation which leads individuals to seek out an appropriate explanation and label for otherwise ambiguous feeling states.

It is illustrative of the paradigm shift that this prominent motivational feature of Schachter's earlier work on affiliation (1959), and the initial research on emotional states (e.g., Schachter & Singer, 1962) has now receded very much into the background. Thus, although it is Schachter's work from which the majority of the contributions in this volume most directly de ive, none of them assigns a central role to any such motivational concept. The only two chapters which do utilize such a construct come from outside the Schachter tradition: the O'Neal chapter on the halo effect (chapter 3), which employs the "need for certainty" proposed by Mills (1968), and the chapter on paranoid delusions by

Maher (chapter 7), in which the postulated intensity and strangeness of the paranoid individual's perceptions motivate him to search for a "rational" reality to account for them.

The third relevant conceptual development has been the theory of self-perception (Bem, 1965, 1972), which states that individuals attribute beliefs, attitudes, and internal states to themselves partially by inferring them from observations of their own overt behavior and/or the circumstances in which it occurs. Thus, according to this theory, when information from internal cues is weak, ambiguous, or uninterpretable, the individual is functionally in the same position as an outside observer of his behavior, an observer who, necessarily, must rely upon those same external cues to infer the individual's inner states. Although this set of hypotheses was originally derived from the "radical-behavioral" analysis of self-referring statements made by B.F. Skinner (1953, 1957), this parentage has been increasingly muted in successive translations of the theory. (For an extended discussion of this historical sequence, see Bem, 1972). The theory itself lacks any motivational construct other than an implicit assumption that individuals are willing to answer inquiries concerning their internal states.

Self-perception theory became an element in the paradigm shift through the proposal that it could incorporate the major phenomena of cognitive dissonance theory (Festinger, 1957) within it (Bem, 1967). Such a reinterpretation removes a major motivational process, dissonance reduction, and replaces it with the nonmotivational, information-processing construct of self-attribution.

The convergence of self-perception theory and the domain of "feeling states" has come about in several ways. First, the theory itself treats all self-descriptions of "private events," including attitudes, emotions, and physiological states, as a single equivalence class insofar as the basic self-observation postulate is concerned. Second, many of the findings emerging from the Schachter tradition can be viewed as special cases of the underlying assumptions of the theory (Bem, 1970, 1972; Nisbett and Valins, 1971). Finally, explicit contact with "feeling states" was achieved through an experiment specifically designed to show that the perception of pain can be partially a function of self-observation (Bandler, Madaras, and Bem, 1968; see also Corah and Boffa, 1970; and Klemp and Leventhal in this volume, chapter 12).

The fourth major development in the move to the attribution paradigm is attribution theory itself. Once again history begins with Heider, who stated the major ideas in *The Psychology of Interpersonal Relations* (1958). During the "consistency" era, this book was cited primarily for its formal balance theory, while Heider's rich but less formalized observations about person perception and attribution were relatively ignored. This was remedied in 1965 by Jones and Davis, who added several testable propositions and explicated some specific empirical consequences of the attribution hypotheses contained within the book. The resulting research tended to focus on an observer's attribution of an actor's intentions and attitudes (e.g., Jones and Harris, 1967) and would probably have proceeded independently of the other three traditions discussed above had it not been for the influential essay, "Attribution Theory in Social Psychology" by Harold Kelley in the 1967 *Nebraska Symposium on Motivation*. This essay integrated the Jones and Davis formulation and the self-perception theory (Bem, 1965) into a single theoretical framework along with some striking propositions about attributional biases, errors, and illusions. These last considerations also afforded Kelley the opportunity to make some perceptive observations about attributional aspects of dissonance experiments, thereby providing an added flourish to the convergence of these several distinct lines of research and theory.

If Kelley can be seen as a final step in this shift from drive models to information-processing models, as this brief intellectual history implies, then it is somewhat ironic that his essay appears in a symposium on motivation. For despite Kelley's valiant try, the motivational flavor is very bland indeed:

> Consideration of attribution theory is relevant for a symposium on motivation in several respects. The theory describes processes that operate *as if* the individual were motivated to attain a cognitive mastery of the causal structure of his environment. Indeed,

Heider explicitly assumes that 'we try to make sense out of the manifold of proximal stimuli...' And Jones and Davis state, 'The perceiver seeks to find sufficient reason why the person acted and why the act took on a particular form.' This broad motivational assumption makes little difference in the development and application of the theory, but it gives the theory a definite functionalistic flavor... and affords whatever motivational basis might seem necessary to support the complex cognitive processes entailed in attribution.

More important for the student of motivation are the specific processes and their consequences. Attribution processes are assumed to instigate, under certain conditions, such activities as information-seeking, communication, and persuasion. Thus attribution theory plays an important role in describing the motivational conditions for these significant classes of social behavior. Equally important is the relevance of attribution theory to the *perception* of motivation, both in others and in one's self...(Kelley, 1967:193; emphasis in the original.)

It is an admirable attempt, but the strongest motivation to emerge from this quotation appears to be Kelley's need to understand why he was there. Presumably his fellow participants were thus provided with "sufficient reason why the person acted and why the act took on a particular form."

This, then, is the surrounding context within which the contributions to this volume can be viewed. We turn next to some of the theoretical issues that recent empirical results have raised for these paradigms and the theories within them.

NONCOGNITIVE RESPONSE CLASSES

If we have managed to alter an individual's attitude or self-attribution, it is not unreasonable to expect that this will induce consequent changes in other response systems. For example, if we have increased a person's favorability toward a dull task, he might be expected to work at the task more assiduously. Make him think he is angry, he should act more aggressively. Change his perception of his hunger, thirst, or pain, and he should consume more or less food or drink, or endure more or less aversive stimulation. Nor should such expectations be confined to instrumental or consummatory behaviors only, for there is a long history of evidence that beliefs, attitudes, and self-attributions can exercise influence over physiological responses. (For reviews, see Frank, 1961, and Zimbardo, 1969.) It is therefore not unreasonable to expect physiological changes to follow upon induced self-attributions of feeling states.

Happily, the experimental laboratory has blessed such expectations with some striking confirmations. Dissonance manipulations designed to enhance the perceived attractiveness of dull tasks do produce greater intensity of behavior on the task itself (for a review, see Weick, 1967). Behavioral observations of subjects in Schachter's experiments reveal them to be behaving "appropriately" in accord with their induced emotional states (e.g., Schachter and Singer, 1962; Schachter and Wheeler, 1962); and dissonance manipulations designed to alter self-attributions of drive states such as hunger, thirst, and pain do alter overt behaviors with respect to their respective stimuli and do produce striking physiological changes (Zimbardo, 1969). In the present volume, we learn that false feedback designed to manipulate self-attributions of anger produces changes in overt instrumental aggression (Berkowitz and Turner, chapter 13), and false feedback designed to create misattributions of higher autonomic arousal induces greater resistance to extinction of the GSR (Koenig and Henriksen, chapter 5).

Precisely because it has been "not unreasonable to expect" these phenomena to occur, and precisely because they have in fact occurred, the problematic nature of their conceptual status within the various theories has been insufficiently appreciated. Thus the "theoretical" predictions or explanations of these phenomena that one finds in print are rarely more sophisticated than the "it-is-not-unreasonable-to-expect..." statement with which this section opened two paragraphs above. The lucky theory within which the particular investigator is working then gets gratuitous credit for the "derivation". A related practice, also encouraged by the fact that the response classes seem to "hang together," is to treat the response classes interchangeably as if they were functionally equivalent; the self-attributions and the noncognitive responses are simply grouped together as the "effects" of the stimulus manipulations. Such practices are unfortunate for they can easily obscure important gaps in our understanding by causing us to pretend to knowledge that we do not in fact possess. It is thus important to explore how the various theories account for these noncognitive response classes.

In attribution models generally--and in the author's self-perception theory in particular--cognitions or self-attributions are the dependent variables. Instrumental behaviors, consummatory responses, and physiological responses (real or falsified) are among the variables that can serve as antecedent or independent variables, the stimuli from which self-attributions of beliefs, attitudes, or feeling states can be partially inferred by the individual. Attribution models are thus very explicit about the direction of the causal arrow, and they remain mute about any phenomenon in which the noncognitive response classes play the dependent variable role; as dependent variables, such response classes are extra-theoretical. To state this another way, attribution models do not treat cognitions, overt behaviors, and physiological responses as functionally equivalent response classes, but rather, spell out in detail the mechanisms by which the cognitive response class can be under the partial functional control of the other two. How do attributional models account for noncognitive response classes? They do not.

The consistency paradigm is in much the same position as the attribution paradigm with regard to the physiological response class. Thus an early prediction that physiological phenomena might emerge from dissonance-theory settings was precisely a speculation in the spirit of "it would not be unreasonable to expect..." (Brehm and Cohen, 1962:151-155). The positive empirical results which followed and confirmed that early hunch (Zimbardo, 1969) in no way altered the theoretical status of the hypothesis within the formal theory itself, nor does the invocation of dissonance reduction as a motivational explanatory concept bridge the gap from the attribution changes to the physiological effects. For example, it is no "explanation" to assert that an individual alters some physiological response in order to "reduce dissonance" until it is explained just how he goes about doing that. This gap is not to be confused with the prior gap from the stimulus operations to the attribution changes, a link with which the theory is prepared to deal. This is, then, the same position in which self-perception theory finds itself (Bem, 1967); it, too, has a theory about the first link, but is reduced to hand-waving about the second.

Similarly, the GSR effects reported in this volume by Koenig and Henriksen (chapter 5) are intriguing and potentially important in their implications for the conditioning therapies as these authors suggest. But the effects are not accounted for by any of the three theories they mention--modeling, Schachter's theory, or self-perception theory--and for the same reason, that is, that none of these theories contains the theoretical machinery for explaining physiological changes in a nontrivial way. For example, the "explanation" borrowed from Schachter's formulation, that "a state of arousal will be perceived as positive or negative depending upon the label that a person attaches to that state, and that he will then behave accordingly," (i.e., show higher resistance to extinction of the GSR) is pure verbal legerdemain. At most, it is a restatement of the data.

It is thus an important step forward simply to recognize that a detailed theoretical model is still needed to account for the cognitive control of physiological responses. One of the criteria for a successful theory in this domain will almost certainly be its ability to account simultaneously for the related physiological effects of placebo medication, hypnotically or cognitively induced anesthesia (cf. Spanos, Barber, and Lang, chapter 11), and associated phenomena of the "mind-body" problem. A start in this direction is provided by Zimbardo (1969) whose theoretical discussion at least outdistances the dissonance-theory framework that guided the choice of stimulus manipulations.

When one turns from the physiological to the behavioral variables associated with the cognitive alteration of feeling states, the consistency paradigm appears to be on firmer ground. For example, although the theory of cognitive dissonance, in literal terms, is a theory about cognitions (like the attribution models), the concept of a general drive toward consistency extends itself more easily to instrumental behaviors than it does to physiological responses. Thus if an individual suffers inconsistency between something he believes and the cognition that he is not behaving in accord with that belief, a purely cognitive conflict, then it follows from the basic postulate of the consistency model that he can achieve drive reduction by altering either the belief or the behavior. The motivational construct within the theory provides a built-in "motor" force behind a change in overt behavior.[1] If a dissonance manipulation makes an individual more favorable toward a dull task, a higher rate of performance on the task is a legitimate prediction from the theory. It is important to note that the behavior, in this formulation, is necessarily mediated by a prior belief, attitude, cognition, or attribution with which the behavior is brought into harmony.

A similar kind of consistency principle is also invoked to explain behavioral effects by many investigators who employ Schachter's theory of emotional states. As already noted above, Koenig and Henricksen (chapter 5) remark that Schachter postulates that an individual "will then behave accordingly" after he has labeled his emotional state. Similarly, Berkowitz and Turner (chapter 13) interpret Schachter as saying that an individual interprets his state and "then acts in a manner consistent with this interpretation." And although Berkowitz and Turner go beyond the Schachter formulation in their own analysis of the stimulus variables leading to instrumental aggression, they too come back to the same mechanism in order to get from the self-attribution of anger to the act of aggression: "Looked at from a larger perspective, the findings also provide yet another demonstration of the search for cognitive consistency. We want our actions to be in accord with our emotions, as we understand them..."

Interestingly, however, Schachter himself does not invoke such a principle of consistency in his own writings on the topic (including Schachter, 1964, which other writers most frequently cite in this connection). Rather, he treats self-attributions and overt behaviors as separate "indices" of the underlying "mood" he set about to produce; that is, Schachter's conceptual analysis treats the two response classes as functionally equivalent. Thus from the very beginning, Schachter and his colleagues have routinely collected behavioral observations along with, or even in lieu of self-report data of emotional state (e.g., Schachter and Singer, 1962; Schachter and Wheeler, 1962). Similarly, self-attributions of hunger appear in some of the obesity studies (e.g., Goldman, Jaffa, and Schachter, 1968), but the dependent variable has now become eating behavior per se, and the word "hunger" has faded quietly from view (cf. Nisbett and Storms, chapter 14). And although several new conceptual distinctions have been introduced into this important research to keep abreast of the new findings, there has been no comparable conceptual distinction introduced to parallel or accompany the sub rosa shifts from one response class to another.

To summarize, pure attribution models presume only to deal with the cognitive response class; additional machinery must be added if they are to deal with behavioral or physiological responses as dependent variables. Schachter's model, hovering somewhere between the information-processing/attribution paradigm and the motivational/drive paradigm, does not distinguish on the dependent-variable side between the self-attributions and the "emotional" behavior. Just as the attribution models do, Schachter's model places physiological responses only in the role of independent variables; they are stimuli which partially determine the individual's perception of his emotional state. Finally, theories within the motivational/drive paradigm, particularly the theory of cognitive dissonance, do not handle the physiological response class in any nontrivial way, but they do have a conceptual device for predicting or explaining any overt behavioral changes that are mediated by prior cognitions, attitudes, or attributions. We turn now to a closer examination of this proposed sequence of events from stimulus manipulation to attribution change to behavior change.

DO ATTRIBUTIONS MEDIATE BEHAVIOR?

Increase a person's favorability toward a dull task, and he will work at it more assiduously. Make him think he is angry, and he will act more aggressively. Change his perception of hunger, thirst, or pain, and he should consume more or less food or drink, or endure more or less aversive stimulation. Alter the attribution, according to the theory, and "consistent" overt behavior will follow.

There seems to be only one snag: it appears not to be true. It is not that the behavioral effects sometimes fail to occur as predicted; that kind of negative evidence rarely embarrasses anyone. It is that they occur more easily, more strongly, more reliably, and more persuasively than the attribution changes that are, theoretically, supposed to be mediating them.

For example, in a well-controlled study by Grinker (1969:127) on eyelid conditioning, it was predicted that "... the dissonance aroused by voluntary commitment to a painful stimulus will be reduced by lowering pain-avoidance motivation, that is, by perceiving the UCS to be less threatening or painful, and thus the conditioning level [will be less]." The study did obtain the predicted effects in conditioning, but "there were no significant differences between any groups on self-report measures of perceived pain, irritability, eye tearing, or apprehension, or on other questionnaire items designed to measure subjective response to the aversive aspects of the situation" (Grinker, 1969:132). And in a closely related experiment, Zimbardo, Cohen, Weisenberg, Dworkin, and Firestone (1969) were able to obtain predicted changes in learning performance, physiological measures, and pain perception. But the attributions of pain showed the weakest effects, and furthermore, the correlations between these cognitive attributions and the behavioral measures of learning that they were supposed to be mediating were -0.01 for one group and +0.11 for the other.

In another kind of study of pain, involving quite different manipulations from the above studies, Davison and Valins (1969) found, as predicted, that experimental subjects were willing to take more shock than control subjects, but they did not rate a set of sample shocks as any less painful than did controls. A study on fear gives similar results. Valins and Ray (1967) asked snake-phobic subjects to look at slides picturing snakes; subjects were given false feedback about their heartbeat rate designed to imply that they were not afraid of snakes. Subsequently these subjects were able to approach the snake more closely than control subjects, but they did not report themselves to be any less frightened of snakes than did the controls.

Finally, Weick (1967) reviewed all studies designed to increase an individual's favorability toward a dull task. He found that increased effort on the task often occurred in the absence of the attitude change toward the task which was supposed to cause the increased effort. Weick concludes (1967:200) that

> initial cognitive enhancement of the task followed by increased effort simply does not occur often enough for us to be convinced that this is a reasonable explanation. Instead, it appears that the phenomenon in which we are interested may involve just the opposite sequence of events, namely behavioral change followed by occasional attempts to summarize the experience evaluatively.

What is one to make of such failures? Unfortunately, it is not yet possible to construct a satisfactory answer to this question. One possible explanation for them is that the measures of attributions are not well-designed or appropriate to the self-attribution which actually mediates the behavior. Another possibility is that subjects are hesitant to admit to some states like anger (Schachter and Singer, 1962). Although these methodological explanations may account for some of the negative findings, the same pattern of results--behavior changes in the absence of equally strong attribution changes--is found in some of the best designed and carefully executed experiments in the field (e.g., Grinker, 1969).

Another possibility is that the attributions do change as predicted and do mediate the behaviors, but that the attributions themselves are unconscious (Brock and Grant, 1963; Zimbardo, 1969:76). There have been arguments, of course, that inconsistency itself and the process of inconsistency reduction need not be represented in awareness (e.g., Tannenbaum, 1968), and the author himself has made a parallel claim that individuals need not be able to verbalize the cues they use in arriving at self-attributions (Bem, 1965, 1968). But such claims can edge dangerously close to metaphysics, and the next retreat into invisibility--that one of the "dissonant" cognitions itself is unknown to the individual--should surely be resisted mightily until all other alternatives, save angels perhaps, have been eliminated. A related but more plausible explanation involving defensive denial processes has been proposed by Zimbardo (1969:269-273); his version of an unconscious cognition at least generates some empirical consequences, and there are some suggestive supporting data for such a process within the settings explored in that body of research.

A final lead is provided by Weick's suggestion, quoted above, that the attributions or attitudes may follow upon rather than precede the behaviors. This is, of course, the major postulate of self-perception theory and a phenomenon well known to dissonance theory. If this is, in fact, the sequence involved, then it would explain why the measured attribution changes are often less reliable and weaker than the behavioral changes, since they are the third, rather than the second link in the chain, as originally assumed. For example, the self-reports of euphoria and anger in the classic Schachter and Singer (1962) experiment were obtained after the behavior had occurred and were, in fact, less reliable than the behavioral observations themselves.

A similar instance appears in the Berkowitz-Turner study (chapter 13). The self-reports of anger were retrospective measures in which the subjects had to recall how angry they had been before engaging in the aggressive behavior. A study by Bem and McConnell (1970) would imply that such "recall" measures would be more highly correlated with the subject's current attribution (as altered by the intervening behavior) than they would be with the actual previous state that he is attempting to recall. And in fact, the Berkowitz-Turner self-report data designed to check the false feedback manipulation of anger do appear to parallel the overt aggression displayed by the subjects more closely than they correspond to the meter readings themselves. Prophetically, Berkowitz himself has said elsewhere: "We generally assume as a matter of course that the human being acts as he does because of wants arising from his understanding of his environment. In some cases, however, this understanding may develop after stimuli have evoked the action so that the understanding justifies but has not caused the behavior" (1968:308).

Is, then, the Berkowitz-Turner study one of these cases of reverse sequence? Not necessarily, for it is still possible that the appropriate attributions were actually present before the behavior and did mediate it. All that can be said is that self-report measures collected after the behavior has occurred may not be a valid index of those attributions. The same holds true for the Schachter-Singer study (1962) and several others that have collected attribution data confounded by intervening behavior. This analysis, then, implies that some of the failures to find attribution changes may simply reflect the methodological practice of collecting the self-reports after other stimulus events, including overt behaviors, have intervened. But like the other explanations offered above, this cannot account for all the failures, for some of the best studies are not subject to this criticism (e.g., Zimbardo et al., 1969), and they still do not find attribution effects as strong as the behavioral ones that they are supposed to be mediating.

If we are thus forced to the conclusion that, at least in some settings, attribution changes do not mediate the observed behavioral effects, then we find that a phenomenon that had been previously accounted for within the consistency paradigm has become "unsolved". That is, we are still left with the task of accounting for the behavior changes themselves. Several attempts to do so are already under way.

For example, Valins (chapter 9) has proposed that the stimulus manipulations themselves may be insufficient actually to alter the attribution, but that they do cause the individual to question his current attribution sufficiently so that he "tests" the new attributional hypothesis by engaging in behavior to find out. As a result of engaging in the behavior, the hypothesis about his attribution may be confirmed, and he will accept the attribution as valid. Or the hypothesis may be disconfirmed, leading him to reject the attribution, and leaving us with a set of results showing a behavioral effect and no attribution effect. Thus false feedback implying that one is not afraid of snakes is not sufficient to create a stable attribution of "I'm not afraid," but it is sufficient to motivate a test of this possibility by approaching the snake. The process of handling the snake can then stabilize the new attribution via the self-perception process. Nisbett and Valins (1971) have spelled out this intriguing scenario in greater detail elsewhere.

With regard to the task enhancement studies, Weick (1967) has suggested that the behavioral effects in these experiments might be accounted for by propositions drawn from frustration theory or cue-utilization theory if we assume that greater frustration and/or arousal is produced by the manipulations in the "high dissonance" conditions. These theories would predice greater intensity of instrumental behavior under higher arousal. Again, the attribution effects--when they do occur--can be handled as post-behavior phenomena by either self-perception theory or dissonance theory.

It may be that still other cases of behavioral effects will be "re-solved" by using variations of motivational constructs like the need to be in control of one's self and environment (cf. deCharms, 1968; Zimbardo, 1969). And, as suggested, the physiological effects should probably be split off and reunited with other physiological phenomena under cognitive influence, rather than being grouped according to their independent-variable manipulations as dissonance or attribution phenomena.

It is clear that the door has now been opened for many minitheories, for it is unlikely that any single process will account for the diverse phenomena that were grouped together when consistency and attribution models converged. It may seem a shame to abandon the parsimony which obtained during the reign of the consistency theories, but it now appears that at least some of that parsimony was illusory and was purchased at the cost of obscuring some important gaps in our knowledge. The fact that everything seems to be falling apart should probably be taken as an index of scientific advance.

STRATEGY OF FUNCTIONAL ANALYSIS

The author's self-perception theory was originally formulated within the framework of radical behaviorism (Bem, 1964), a framework comprising a particular set of conceptual strategies for approaching behavioral phenomena. Known as functional analysis, this approach addresses complex behavioral phenomena by inquiring first into the ontogenetic origins of the observed dependent variables, treated as response classes in their own right rather than as reflections of underlying structures, processes, or internal states, and then attempts to ascertain the controlling or independent stimulus variables of which those observable behaviors are a function. The distinguishing features of this strategy are spelled out in greater detail in Bem (1972), and it is sufficient to note here that the stubborn functional orientation can bestow some heuristic advantages that no other approach can provide whenever--as in the current case--behavioral mysteries threaten to become behavioral-science muddles.

Thus, if there is an underlying moral to the discussion in previous sections, it is that response classes should be given independent conceptual status, one from the other, and analyzed separately for the stimulus variables that control them. If they covary, we should first inspect the stimulus manipulations for overlapping functional properties that produce that covariance. Any theory that assumes that one response class should vary as a function of another (as self-perception theory does) ought to spell out in detail the mechanism of control. What are the stimulus properties of the response class that are presumed to exert functional control over the other? Finally, response classes should not be treated as functionally equivalent unless the theory explicitly dictates that they can be and/or experimentation vindicates the merger.

Orthodox radical behaviorists are not the only psychologists whose analyses are informed by these tactics. For example, Leventhal (1970) has recently employed a similar strategy in analyzing the attitudinal and behavioral effects of fear-arousing communications, thereby bringing elegant order out of the chaotic and conflicting findings in this area. (In addition, Leventhal's analysis is another instance of a drive theory being replaced by an information-processing orientation.) Berkowitz's analysis of aggression (1965; Berkowitz and Turner, chapter 13) has a similar functional spirit and strategy behind it.

If adopted generally, such a strategy would also lead to very different kinds of analyses within the domain of feeling states. For example, Schachter's own review of the literature on emotion (1964) reveals that physiological cues should have more functional control over feeling state attributions than over "emotional" behaviors per se. Thus sympathectomized animals continue to show emotional behavior, and human "subjects with cervical lesions described themselves as acting emotional but not feeling emotional" (Schachter, 1964:74). These findings would seem to have implications for which response class is being used as the "index" of mood in the Schachter experiments. But as noted earlier, Schachter and his colleagues interchange the two response classes repeatedly and nowhere acknowledge a functional distinction between them.

The divergence between the two response classes would have emerged even more explicitly in the obesity work if investigators had continued to gather both observations of eating behavior and self-reports of hunger, for the two response classes now appear to covary "hardly at all" (Richard E. Nisbett, personal communication, August 19, 1971). It is apparently fortuitous that attention in the obesity work has shifted to eating behavior as such, for this does appear to be where the action is, even if the action leads out of social psychology (see Nisbett and Storms, chapter 14). Indeed, these points about the conceptual treatment of different response classes are not intended as criticism of this important research.

A similar confounding of these same response classes appears in an experiment on insomnia by Storms and Nisbett (1970), an experiment also conducted within the Schachter framework. Insomniacs were given the placebo pills and told either that the pills would produce arousal or relaxation. The subjects were asked to report how long it took them to get to sleep following the medication. As predicted, "arousal" subjects reported that they got to sleep more quickly than they had on nights without the pills, presumably because they attributed their arousal to the pills rather than to their emotions, and as a consequence worried less about their insomnia, a worry which seems to exacerbate the problem. Also as predicted, "relaxed" subjects reported that they got to sleep less quickly than usual, presumably because they assumed that their emotions were unusually intense because their arousal level was high even after taking an arousal-reducing agent.

The important point to note here is that the dependent variable is the subject's report of how much time had passed before he fell asleep, itself an attribution statement. But when this experiment is cited, and even in the abstract of the article itself, it is reported that "arousal" subjects got to sleep more quickly and "relaxation" subjects got to sleep less quickly. And that is not the same thing. Estimates of time passage are themselves attributions that are subject to manipulation (cf. London and Monello, chapter 6). Perhaps the implied state of arousal is more interesting to introspect than the implied state of relaxation, making time appear to pass more quickly. If true, then "arousal" subjects would report getting to sleep more quickly even if it were not true. This alternative explanation is admittedly less plausible than the original, but the point to be made here is that the time it takes to fall asleep is a different response measure from the self-report of the time it takes to fall asleep, and both are subject to cognitive manipulations. Indeed, the therapeutic implications of this experiment could be quite different from those suggested by the authors unless we are prepared to assume that getting insomniacs to think they are falling asleep faster is the same as curing insomnia.

Finally, consider the study by Koenig and Henriksen (chapter 5) on GSR extinction. A functional analysis would first note that the dependent variable is a member of a response class known to be subject to classical conditioning procedures. Thus, all independent variables should be examined for their arousal or conditioned-stimulus properties. For example, Spence and Goldstein (1961) have shown that even verbal threats lead to increased strength of classical conditioning. This prompts the question of whether giving a subject (false) information that he is aroused, as Koenig and Henriksen do, might not have the same effect as an oral threat and thus increase resistance to extinction. This functional analysis suggests that it is irrelevant that the independent variable happened also to be informational feedback about the subject's alleged arousal. Indeed, the control group that watched the feedback meter without knowing what it meant was probably less relevant to the experiment than a control group of subjects who thought it was an index of halitosis.

For years, personality theory has been dominated by the "trait" assumption that there are pervasive cross-situational consistencies in an individual's behavior. After reviewing the literature, Mischel (1968) concludes that the empirical search for such consistencies or traits rarely generates a correlation above +.30, a finding of some disappointment if one's theory of human behavior anticipates +1.00. He suggests a learning-theoretic functional analysis in which covariance of responses is sought in the overlap of situational conditions which evoke and maintain particular response classes. Under such a strategy, we construct the consistencies from the ground up rather than assuming them a priori, and any increment over zero in the magnitude of the cross-situational correlations becomes an occasion for some rejoicing.

There is a parallel in social psychology. The decade of the consistency theories has been dominated by the assumption that everything was glued together until proved otherwise. Since it is now proving otherwise, it is suggested that we try the opposite assumption that nothing is glued together until proved otherwise. It is a question of whether we should begin with expectations of +1.00 correlations or 0.00 correlations. The heuristic advantage of this strategy is not guaranteed, of course. But the difference in morale if +.30 correlations continue to come in is itself worth considering.

NOTE

1. Note that we thus grant legitimacy to a motivational concept for explaining cognitive and behavioral responses, but deny it legitimacy in accounting for physiological responses. The distinction, however, is not based upon response class membership per se, but upon the individual's ability to control directly the response. A motivational construct is still, at bottom, a way of saying that the individual "wants to" perform some response, even if unconsciously; being motivated is not

sufficient, however, if he "doesn't know which string to pull." As recent work demonstrates, physiological responses can be brought under direct conscious control; presumably they then become subject to motivational expectations in the same way that instrumental responses such as lifting one's finger do. Nevertheless, we are still avoiding the deeper epistemological problems concerning the explanatory legitimacy of motivational constructs generally. As a sometimes radical behaviorist, I am inclined to the view that their explanatory power is, in general, illusory.

REFERENCES

Abelson, R.P. Aronson, E., McGuire, W.J., Newcomb, T.M., Rosenberg, M.J., and Tannenbaum, P.H. (eds.). 1968. *Theories of Cognitive Consistency: A Sourcebook*. Chicago: Rand McNally.

Bandler, R.J., Madaras, G.R., and Bem, D.J. 1968. Self-observation as a source of pain perception. *Journal of Personality and Social Psychology* 9:205-209.

Bem, D.J. 1964. An experimental analysis of beliefs and attitudes. Dissertation, University of Michigan, Ann Arbor: University Microfilms, 64-12:558.

----. 1965. An experimental analysis of self-persuasion. *Journal of Experimental Social Psychology* 1: 100-218.

----. 1967. Self-perception: An alternative interpretation of cognitive dissonance phenomena. *Psychological Review* 74:183-200.

----. 1968. Attitudes as self-descriptions: Another look at the attitude-behavior link. *In* A. C. Greenwald, T.C. Brock, and T.M. Ostrom (eds.), *Psychological Foundations of Attitudes*. New York: Academic Press.

----. 1970. *Beliefs, Attitudes, and Human Affairs*. Belmont: Brooks/Cole.

----. 1972. Self-perception theory. *In* L. Berkowitz (ed.), *Advances in Experimental Social Psychology*, Vol. 6. New York: Academic Press.

Bem, D.J., and McConnell, H.K. 1970. Testing the self-perception explanation of dissonance phenomena: On the salience of premanipulation attitudes. *Journal of Personality and Social Psychology* 14:23-31.

Berkowitz, L. 1965. The concept of aggressive drive: Some additional considerations. *In* L. Berkowitz (ed.), *Advances in Experimental Social Psychology*, Vol. 2. New York: Academic Press, 301-329.

----. 1968. The motivational status of cognitive consistency theorizing. *In* R.P. Abelson et al. (eds.), *Theories of Cognitive Consistency: A Sourcebook*. Chicago: Rand McNally.

Brehm, J.W., and Cohen, A.R. 1962. *Explorations in Cognitive Dissonance*. New York: Wiley.

Brock, T.C., and Grant, L.D. 1963. Dissonance, awareness, and motivation. *Journal of Abnormal and Social Psychology* 67:53-60.

Corah, N.L., and Boffa, J. 1970. Perceived control, self-observation, and response to aversive stimulation. *Journal of Personality and Social Psychology* 16:1-4.

Davison, G.C., and Valins, S. 1969. Maintenance of self-attributed and drug-attributed behavior change. *Journal of Personality and Social Psychology* 11:25-33.

deCharms, R. 1968. *Personal Causation: The Internal Affective Determinants of Behavior*. New York: Academic Press.

Festinger, L. 1954. A theory of social comparison processes. *Human Relations* 7:117-140.

----. 1957. *A Theory of Cognitive Dissonance*. Stanford: Stanford University Press.

Frank, J. 1961. *Persuasion and Healing*. Baltimore: Johns Hopkins Press.

Goldman, R., Jaffa, M., and Schachter, S. 1968. Yom Kippur, Air France, dormitory food, and the eating behavior of obese and normal persons. *Journal of Personality and Social Psychology* 10:117-123.

Grinker, J. 1969. Cognitive control of classical eyelid conditioning. *In* P.G. Zimbardo (ed.), *The Cognitive Control of Motivation*. Glenview, Ill.: Scott, Foresman.

Heider, F. 1946. Attitudes and cognitive organizations. *Journal of Psychology* 21:107-112.

----. 1958. *The Psychology of Interpersonal Relations*. New York: Wiley.

----. 1960. The gestalt theory of motivation. *In* M.R. Jones (ed.), *Nebraska Symposium on Motivation,* Vol. 8. Lincoln: University of Nebraska Press, 145-172.

Jones, E.E., and Davis, K.E. 1965. From acts to dispositions. *In* L. Berkowitz (ed.), *Advances in Experimental Social Psychology,* Vol. 2. New York: Academic Press, 219-266.

Jones, E.E., and Harris, V.A. 1967. The attribution of attitudes. *Journal of Experimental Social Psychology* 3:1-24.

Kelley, H.H. 1967. Attribution theory in social psychology. *In* D. Levine (ed.), *Nebraska Symposium on Motivation,* Vol. 15. Lincoln: University of Nebraska Press, 192-238.

Leventhal, H. 1970. Findings and theory in the study of fear communications. *In* L. Berkowitz (ed.), *Advances in Experimental Social Psychology,* Vol. 5. New York: Academic Press, 120-186.

McGuire, W.J. 1966. The current status of cognitive consistency theories. *In* S. Feldman (ed.), *Cognitive Consistency: Motivational Antecedents and Behavioral Consequents*. New York: Academic Press, 1-46.

Mills, J. 1968. Interest in supporting and discrepant information. *In* R.P. Abelson et al. (eds.), *Theories of Cognitive Consistency: A Sourcebook*. Chicago: Rand McNally, 771-776.

Mischel, W. 1968. *Personality and Assessment*. New York: Wiley.

Nisbett, R.E., and Valins, S. 1971. Perceiving the causes of one's own behavior. *In* E.E. Jones, D.E. Kanouse, H.H. Kelley, R.E. Nisbett, S. Valins, and B. Weiner, (eds.), *Attribution: Perceiving the Causes of Behavior*. New York: General Learning Press.

Schachter, S. 1959. *The Psychology of Affiliation*. Stanford: Stanford University Press.

----. 1964. The interaction of cognitive and physiological determinants of emotional state. *In* L. Berkowitz (ed.), *Advances in Experimental Social Psychology,* Vol. 1. New York: Academic Press, 49-80.

Schachter, S., and Singer, J.E. 1962. Cognitive, social, and physiological determinants of emotional state. *Psychological Review* 69:379-399.

Schachter, S., and Wheeler, L. 1962. Epinephrine, chlorpromazine and amusement. *Journal of Abnormal and Social Psychology* 65:121-128.

Skinner, B.F. 1953. *Science and Human Behavior.* New York: MacMillan.

----. 1957. *Verbal Behavior.* New York: Appleton-Century-Crofts.

Spence, K.W., and Goldstein, H. 1961. Eyelid conditioning performance as a function of emotion-producing instructions. *Journal of Experimental Psychology* 62:291-294.

Storms, M.D., and Nisbett, R.E. 1970. Insomnia and the attribution process. *Journal of Personality and Social Psychology* 2:319-328.

Tannenbaum, P.A. 1968. The congruity principle: Retrospective reflections and recent research. *In* R. Abelson et al. (eds.), *Theories of Cognitive Consistency: A Sourcebook.* Chicago: Rand McNally, 52-72.

Valins, S., and Ray, A.A. 1967. Effects of cognitive desensitization on avoidance behavior. *Journal of Personality and Social Psychology* 7:345-350.

Weick, K.E. 1967. Dissonance and task enhancement: A problem for compensation theory? *In* M.D. Dunnette, E.E. Lawiter,K.E. Weick, and R.L. Opsahl (eds.), The role of financial compensation in managerial motivation. *Organizational Behavior and Human Performance* 2:175-216.

Zimbardo, P.G. 1969. *The Cognitive Control of Motivation: The Consequences of Choice and Dissonance.* Glenview, Ill.: Scott Foresman.

Zimbardo, P.G., Cohen, A. Weisenberg, M., Dworkin, L., and Firestone, I. 1969. The control of experimental pain. *In* P.G. Zimbardo (ed.), *The Cognitive Control of Motivation.* Glenview, Ill.: Scott, Foresman, 100-125.

Index